Appalachian Trail Guide
MARYLAND AND NORTHERN VIRGINIA

1989
Thirteenth Edition

THE POTOMAC APPALACHIAN TRAIL CLUB
1718 N Street, N.W.
Washington, D.C. 20036

APPALACHIAN TRAIL GUIDE
MARYLAND AND NORTHERN VIRGINIA
Thirteenth Edition edited by
MICHAEL T. SHOEMAKER

Printing History

The area covered in this *Guide* was originally part of a more comprehensive publication known as the *Guide to Paths in the Blue Ridge*. The first version was issued in 1931 and referred to Virginia only. In a second edition in 1934, the area covered was extended to include Pennsylvania and Maryland; supplements were issued in 1935 and 1937. The third edition was published in 1941 and the fourth in 1950. In 1959, the comprehensive guidebook was divided into three sections, one of which covered the area represented by this *Guide*. The sixth through twelfth editions appeared in 1966, 1970, 1972, 1974, 1979, 1984, and 1986 respectively.

Library of Congress Catalog Number 86–62720
ISBN 0915746–33–6

1718 N Street, N.W.
Washington, D.C. 20036

PREFACE

The thirteenth edition of this *Guide* represents a small, but important, revision of the previous edition. The principal changes are the relocation around Linden, affecting Virginia Sections 4 and 5, and the revision of the Elk Ridge Trail (its first in ten years). In addition, smaller relocations occurred in Maryland Section 1 and Virginia Section 2, and new shelters appeared in Virginia Sections 2, 4, and 5. The relocations add up to more than 6.5 miles of new Trail, with a net gain of 0.43 miles in the length of the Trail. These and other changes were scouted and measured by the editor in the winter of 1988–89.

Some hikers have asked why measurements are carried out to hundredths-of-a-mile, instead of just tenths. The primary reason is that it provides greater clarity to the organization of the data. If tenths alone were used, many data entries would have to be combined, resulting in a loss of clarity. There are also a few instances when hundredths may be useful to the hiker. The editor has found, from repeated trials, that his measurements are generally accurate to within plus or minus 0.05 miles per ten miles.

Reports to the PATC of errors or changes will be appreciated. Corrections and new information will be included in the next edition.

—Michael T. Shoemaker
February 19, 1989

ACKNOWLEDGMENTS

To Don Owens, Chris Brunton, and Lee Colyer, for providing updated information about the Trail.

To Kathy Miller and Jean Golightly, for photographs.

To Jean Golightly, for supervising the publication of this edition.

ABBREVIATIONS

AT or Trail	Appalachian Trail
ATC or Conference	Appalachian Trail Conference
mi.	mile or miles
PATC	Potomac Appalachian Trail Club
USGS	U.S. Geological Survey

CONTENTS

Raven Rock, Md.

CHAPTER 1
USE OF THE GUIDE AND THE TRAIL

This *Guide* is one of a series of guidebooks that covers the entire Appalachian Trail *(AT)* from Maine to Georgia. It contains a general description and detailed data in both directions for 98.88 miles of the *AT,* from the Maryland-Pennsylvania border to Shenandoah National Park. A list of other guidebooks for the Trail is included in Chapter 2 and on the back cover.

Disclaimer Notice to All Trail Users and Landowners

Although the editor, the PATC, and the Conference strive for accuracy and thoroughness in the materials published, it is impossible to ensure that all the published information accurately describes the condition and location of the Trail. Consequently, the editor, the PATC and its agents, and the Conference disclaim any liability for inaccuracies published in the guidebook.

The Trail crosses both private and public lands, the owners or administrators of which may alter Trail conditions and impose regulations on the use of the Trail. The editor, the PATC and its agents, and the Conference expressly disclaim any liability for the negligence, wrongful actions or omissions of any landowner with respect to the Trail, and of any Trail users with respect to private or public property.

This guide and associated maps refer to springs as sources of water. The purity of water from any sources cannot be guaranteed, and the editor, the PATC and its agents, and the Conference expressly disclaim liability for any impurities in such water. Extreme care must be used in drinking such water. All water should be purified by boiling, or chemically treated before use, but even these measures will not guarantee the safe use of such water, particularly if the water is chemically polluted. Creeks, rivers, ponds, and lakes should never be used as a water source.

The editor, the PATC and its agents, and the Conference expressly disclaim any liability for the condition of the Trail and for all occurrences on the Trail.

Format of the Guidebook

The format of this *Guide* follows the 1979 *Manual for the Preparation of Appalachian Trail Guides,* published by the ATC. The data are broken down by states, but one chapter is devoted to Harpers Ferry, while the rest of West Virginia has been combined with Virginia because part of the *AT* weaves back and forth across their mutual boundary. Within each state, the data have been broken into sections demarcated by highway crossings or by some geographical feature.

The introductory material for each section is given only once, under the headings "Road Approaches and Parking," "Points of Interest," "Maps," "Shelters," "Public Accommodations," "Supplies" (which includes water, post offices, and telephones), and "Side Trails" (which are merely listed). Headings are omitted when they are not applicable to a section. Because only major highways cross the *AT* in Virginia, no travel directions are given under "Road Approaches" for the Virginia Trail sections. Within each section, the "Brief Description" and "Detailed Trail Data" are presented in both directions. Separate chapters at the end of the *Guide* provide additional information about shelters and major side trails.

The "Detailed Trail Data" heading lists locations in miles. Features listed under the headings are given location references in parentheses, with the north-to-south distance listed first, followed by a slash, followed by the south-to-north distance. A few apparent discrepancies in the location references are actually the result of a feature having a different "starting point," depending upon the direction of travel.

Three degrees of steepness are generally distinguished in the Trail descriptions: "ascend," "ascend steeply," and "ascend very steeply," and similarly for descent. The term "undulating" is used to refer to a rapid series of very slight ascents and descents. The word "ahead" is used to distinguish a feature that is a slight distance farther ahead from the listed location. Hence, "descend" and "descend ahead" do not mean the same thing. The former applies immediately, while the latter does not.

It should be remembered that descriptions can become obsolete very quickly as man or nature alters the landscape. Further, the *AT* is subject to reroutings, especially where it now follows highways or crosses privately owned land.

Trail Maps

Detailed maps of the *AT* are available for the entire area covered by this *Guide*. Their use is highly recommended.

The maps have been prepared by the Maps Committee of the PATC and are based on USGS quadrangles (7½ minutes). They indicate the route of the *AT* (marked in contrasting color), side trails, shelters, cabins, highways, forest areas, and other major geographical features. Relief is shown by contour lines.

Five maps cover the *AT* in Maryland and northern Virginia. Maps #5 and #6 are printed on the same sheet and are priced as one map. The area covered by each is as follows:

Map No.	State	Area
5	Maryland	Pen Mar to Turners Gap
6	Maryland	Interstate 70 to Harpers Ferry
7	Virginia/W. Va.	Harpers Ferry to Snickers Gap
8	Virginia	Snickers Gap to US–522
9	Virginia	US–522 to US–211

In addition, PATC Map A ("The Washington-Baltimore Appalachian Trail Area") provides a general overview of the entire section and is useful in determining highway approaches to the *AT*.

These maps are available for a small charge from PATC Headquarters and various other distributors. The maps, like the *Guide*, are periodically revised. In the Trail descriptions, references to changes and errors apply only to the 1986 edition of Maps #5 and #6, the 1982 edition of Map #7, and the 1985 edition of Map #8.

The relevant PATC map is indicated under "Maps" for each section of the *AT*. Also included is reference to the appropriate USGS quadrangle map. These quadrangles may be purchased for $2.50 each from USGS offices at: F St. between 18th and

19th Sts., N.W., Washington, D.C. 20240; or Box 25286, Mail Stop 306, Denver Federal Center, Denver, CO 80225.

The Trail

Trail Markings

Through most of the area covered by this *Guide,* the *AT* is marked by white paint blazes and standardized plaques. In Harpers Ferry, however, the Park Service has banned markings in the town streets, and only plaques mark the *AT* route along the cliff.

The paint blazes (2″ by 6″) have been placed at frequent intervals along the Trail. A double blaze (two blazes, one placed above the other) is placed as a warning sign. It may indicate a turn or change in direction that might otherwise not be noticed.

Metal plaques with the *AT* insignia are placed at greater intervals. Maintained side trails are marked by blue blazes similar in size to the white blazes.

Important intersections are marked with wooden signs.

Trail Maintenance

The PATC is responsible for maintaining about 235 miles of *AT,* as well as blue-blazed side trails, from Pine Grove Furnace State Park in Pennsylvania through Shenandoah National Park. Within Maryland, PATC has assigned Sections 1 and 2 to the Mountain Club of Maryland (Baltimore), and Section 3 to Maryland Appalachian Trail Club of Hagerstown. In any case, all maintenance work is done by unpaid volunteers, usually with sub-sections assigned to individual overseers.

Trail Use

Although much of the Trail is on public property, some of it still crosses private land. Owners can, and sometimes do, order the *AT* off their property. Where this happens, the alternatives are often limited—sometimes only public highways. It is, therefore, *extremely important that private property rights be respected.*

Those using the *AT* or side trails should not damage natural nor man-made property, litter, carry firearms, nor use trail bikes. Particular care should be taken to avoid fires. Smoking is discouraged, and fires should be built only at designated campsites. Camping should be done only at such campsites. Horseback riding requires specific permission of property owners and is forbidden in many areas.

Cabin and Blackburn Trail Center

Bear Spring Cabin, in Maryland Section 5, is the only cabin open to the public within the area covered by this guide. It is a one-room, log structure on 1½ acres of land donated to the PATC in 1939 by Harrison S. Krider. No more than six persons, including children, may use the cabin and surrounding area overnight. The cabin is provided with necessary equipment, including pans, dishes, cutlery, wood stove, blankets, matresses, and bunks, but no lighting sources are available. All the user need bring is personal gear, additional bedding (usually a sleeping bag), lighting sources (flashlights or lanterns), and food. A *spring* and privy are nearby. For access, see Bear Spring Cabin Trail, under "Side Trails," Chapter 7.

The cabin is locked. Arrangements for use, for a small fee, may be made up to three weeks in advance (four weeks for PATC members) by calling Cabin Reservations at PATC Headquarters (area code 202-638-5306) between 7 p.m. and 10 p.m., week-nights only.

The Blackburn Trail Center (see Virginia Section 2) is available for use by PATC members, or groups, for a small fee. Reservations are required, and may be made up to one month in advance, but exclusive use of the Center is not guaranteed. Call Cabin Reservations (see previous paragraph) to make reservations and to obtain information about who will be using the Center on specific dates. The Center has a full-time caretaker from April through September, but is locked at other times. The neighboring Hodgson House has been converted into a primitive cabin that accommodates eight. It has beds and a woodstove, but no mattresses or other equipment. It is open all year and is free to *AT* thru-hikers.

Clothing and Equipment

There are no special requirements for clothing for this section of the Trail. Thunderstorms are fairly frequent throughout the summer, so backpackers are advised to carry a water-repellent jacket, or poncho, and a second set of dry clothes.

Good shoes or boots are important if one is hiking very far. For detailed advice on selecting footwear, see PATC's pamphlet "What Do You Want in a Hiking Shoe?" by Len Wheat.

The amount of equipment needed will vary with the length of the hike. In general, it is advisable to carry at least a map, a compass, a first-aid kit, and a canteen. The latter is particularly useful in hot, dry weather when springs are apt to go dry. During such periods, it is also desirable to carry an insect repellent of some sort.

Poison Ivy, Snakes, and Rabies

Poison Ivy

Poison ivy is found along the Trail and is profuse in some areas, as noted in the Trail descriptions. Poisoning is largely preventable if one knows how to identify the plants. They are usually vines, but in full sunlight may grow as low shrubs. The leaves always consist of three leaflets. Only one three-part leaf leads off from each node on the stem.

The skin irritant of poison ivy is found in all parts of the plant, including roots and fruit. The danger of poisoning is greatest in spring and summer when sap is abundant.

While poisoning usually is caused by contact with some part of the plant, it may also be caused by contact with some intermediate object that has touched a plant, such as clothing, pets, etc.

The time between contamination and first symptoms varies greatly with individuals. They may appear in a few hours or even after 5 days or more. There is no absolute quick cure for all individuals. Prompt washing with cold water may help, and certain lotions can reduce irritation.

For further details on poison ivy, see the following publications, which are sold by the Superintendent of Documents, U.S. Government Printing Office:

Poison Ivy, Poison Oak, and Poison Sumac: Identification, Precautions, Eradication, U.S. Department of Agriculture, Farmers' Bulletin No. 1972.

Poison Ivy, Oak, and Sumac, Public Health Service, Publication 1723.

Poison Ivy, Public Health Services, FS 2.50: 65/4.

Poisonous Snakes

Two types of poisonous snakes inhabit the area covered by this *Guide:* the copperhead and the timber rattlesnake. Copperheads are rarely more than 3 feet long; they have a coppery-to-dull brown head and pale pinkish or reddish-brown body marked with large cross bands of chestnut brown, resembling dumbbells or hourglasses; the tail is tapered. Timber rattlesnakes are usually 2.5 to 3.5 feet long; they may be yellowish or tan, with chevron-shaped cross bands of black or dull brown, but they are often so dull as to appear entirely black; the tail is either blunt or carries the characteristic rattles. Both snakes have heads that are rather flat on top and that have wide jaws; immediately behind the jaw the neck is much smaller. The body tends to be fat and heavy. Neither is particularly aggressive, but they are dangerous if cornered or surprised.

Although both snakes are among the least venomous and cases of snakebite are relatively uncommon, they are dangerous enough to warrant care on the part of the hiker to avoid them. The most important precaution is not to put your hands or feet into places you cannot see clearly. In particular, avoid piles of rock, wood, or brush. Do not sit on rock walls, and look around before sitting anywhere. Wear high-topped boots. Stay on trails, rather than plunging through underbrush. During cool spells, and in the morning or evening, watch the trail for snakes that may be too sluggish to get out of the way. Do not hike alone.

In case of snakebite, the most important thing is to get medical attention to the victim (or vice versa) as soon, and with as little excitement and exertion by the victim, as possible. Suction with a plastic sucker from a snake-bite kit may be helpful if applied within the first two minutes. If the bite is on an extremity, a wide constricting bandage should be placed above the bite and tightened enough to slow near-surface circulation, but not enough to stop the pulse. It should be loosened every 10 to 15 minutes for a minute or two and should be kept ahead of the swelling as it progresses. In any case, medical attention should always be obtained no matter how minor the bite. Antivenin is useful even if given hours after the bite. Because antivenin may have side effects, it is important to know definitely whether a bite is from a poisonous snake, and to know which species is involved.

Rabies

A recent epidemic of rabies in northern Virginia and Maryland may pose a danger to hikers. The epidemic may well last for several more years.

Though raccoons have been the primary carriers, foxes, dogs, bats, and other mammals are all potential carriers. All wild mammals should be avoided. Animals may carry the disease even though they show no symptoms. Unusual behavior by mammals should be reported to the authorities.

Transmission of rabies can occur from virtually any contact, even indirectly, from an inanimate object. Therefore, a danger is posed by raccoons tampering with packs and equipment. The usual precautions for hanging all equipment, by a rope, from a tree, should be followed.

Medical help should be sought immediately by anyone who believes he, or she, has had contact, direct or indirect, with a rabid animal.

Distress Signal

An emergency call for help consists of three short signals, audible or visible, repeated at regular intervals. A whistle is particularly useful. Visible signals may include: light flashes from a mirror, or smoke puffs, in the daytime; or flashes from a flashlight, or three small steady fires, at night.

Anyone recognizing such a signal should acknowledge it by a signal of two calls and then go to the distressed and determine the nature of the emergency.

Rocky Run Shelter

CHAPTER 2
THE APPALACHIAN TRAIL

The Appalachian Trail is a continuous, marked footpath extending from Mount Katahdin, in the central Maine wilderness, some 2,000 miles south to Springer Mountain in Georgia. It is a skyline route along the crest of the ranges generally referred to as Appalachian; hence the name of the Trail.

Early History

The Appalachian Trail was originally proposed in 1921 by Benton MacKaye, forester and regional planner of Shirley Center, Massachusetts. From his early wanderings in the New England forests, he had conceived the vision of a trail which would be the backbone of mountain recreation in the East. He wrote up his plan in an article, "The Appalachian Trail, An Experiment in Regional Planning," in the October 1921 issue of the *Journal of the American Institute of Architects.*

There was some interest in the New York-New Jersey area; a section was constructed near Bear Mountain in the Palisades Interstate Park. But it was not until 1926, when Arthur Perkins of Hartford, Connecticut, revived the endless footpath idea, that enthusiasm among outdoor groups initiated the inclusion of sections of trail already in use as portions of the Appalachian Trail.

The existing sections included the Appalachian Mountain Club's trails in New England, the Long Trail of the Green Mountain Club in Vermont, and the Dartmouth Outing Club's trail system between the Green Mountains of Vermont and the White Mountains of New Hampshire. With the Bear Mountain and Harriman sections of Palisades Interstate Park in New York, existing trails made up a total of about 350 miles out of the planned 2,000 miles from Maine to Georgia.

In the south, trails in National Forests were developed. Some time later two National Parks, the Great Smoky Mountains and Shenandoah, each contributed some of the most used hiking trails. This was all on publicly owned lands.

The connecting trails, however, would have to be on private land. The trail pioneers worked out routes, mostly along mountain tops for some of the best scenery in the East. Their enthusiasm persuaded land owners to become hosts to the Trail. Generally it was oral permission, quite adequate in the early 1930's. Owners really didn't expect too many folks to want to walk in their mountains.

New clubs were formed to build and maintain the Trail. The U.S. Forest Service and the National Park Service, state parks and forests translated their interest into real assistance.

The Trail Route

The Appalachian Trail traverses fourteen states. From Katahdin in Maine the route leads in a general southwesterly direction across Maine and New Hampshire and into Vermont, where it turns south on the Long Trail along the crest of the Green Mountains to the Massachusetts line. It then follows the highlands in western Massachusetts, has a rather circuitous course in western Connecticut, crosses the Hudson River at Bear Mountain Bridge, and follows close to the New York-New Jersey Line to the base of the Kittatinny Range, which it follows to the Delaware Water Gap. West of the Water Gap it follows the crest of Blue Mountain to Swatara Gap where, to avoid the Edward Martin Military Reservation, it turns northwest. After crossing several ridges and traversing the beautiful St. Anthony's Wilderness, it descends from Peters Mountain to cross the Susquehanna on the Clarks Ferry Bridge.

From the Susquehanna River south, the Trail follows Cove Mountain to near Grier Point, crosses the Cumberland Valley by secondary roads, and then traverses South Mountain through Michaux State Forest in Pennsylvania to Pen Mar. It leads across Maryland to the Potomac River at Weverton, follows the towpath of the Chesapeake and Ohio Canal to Harpers Ferry, and crosses the Potomac and Shenandoah rivers. From the Shenandoah, the Trail in general follows the crest of the Blue Ridge, continuing south through the Shenandoah National Park.

At Rockfish Gap the section maintained by the Potomac Appalachian Trail Club ends. Beyond, the route leads through the George Washington National Forest and the Jefferson National Forest, west of Roanoke. It follows the western rim of the Blue Ridge into Tennessee and North Carolina passing through the Cherokee and Pisgah National Forests and the Great Smoky Mountains National Park. From here it cuts through the Nantahala Mountains in the Nantahala National Forest and in Georgia traverses the Chattahoochee National Forest to Springer Mountain.

The Appalachian Trail Conference

The Appalachian Trail Conference is the parent organization for the overall Trail. It coordinates efforts of trail clubs, federal and state governments, and individuals in trail building, marking and maintenance. The Conference is headquartered in Harpers Ferry, W. Va. 25425 (P.O. Box 807).

The Trail route is divided into six districts with three representatives from each serving on the Board of Managers, the governing body of the Appalachian Trail Conference. Sessions of the Trail Conference are usually held every third year.

The membership consists of organizations which maintain the Trail or contribute to the Trail project, individuals who in either personal or an official capacity are responsible for the maintenance of sections of the Trail, and individual dues-paying members.

Publications

The Conference issues a newsletter, bulletins, and guidebooks.

General news and current comments on the Trail can be found in *Appalachian Trailway News* (free to members of the Conference).

Guidebooks issued by the Conference and/or available through it include:

1. *The Appalachian Trail Guide—Maine*
2. *The Appalachian Trail Guide—New Hampshire and Vermont*
3. *The Appalachian Trail Guide—Massachusetts and Connecticut*

4. *The Appalachian Trail Guide—New York and New Jersey*
5. *The Appalachian Trail Guide—Pennsylvania*
6. *The Appalachian Trail Guide—Maryland and Northern Virginia*
7. *The Appalachian Trail Guide—Shenandoah National Park*
8. *The Appalachian Trail Guide—Central and Southern Virginia*
9. *The Appalachian Trail Guide—Tennessee and North Carolina (Cherokee, Pisgah and Great Smokies)*
10. *The Appalachian Trail Guide—North Carolina (the Great Smokies, the Nantahalas) and Georgia*

A complete list of publications, with current prices, is available from the Conference.

Legislative Developments

The first meeting of the Conference was held in March 1925. In the early years, the primary responsibility of the group was to guide the construction and maintenance of the Trail. Since completion of the Trail in 1937, the Conference has been concerned with maintenance, preserving the continuity of the route, and providing information for those using the Trail.

In 1938 the Conference was instrumental in negotiating the signing of the Appalachian Trailway Agreement by the National Park Service, the U.S. Forest Service, and most of the states through which the Trail runs. It meant that on land under the jurisdiction of Federal agencies, no incompatible development would be permitted within a zone of one mile on either side of the Appalachian Trail. (The states subscribed to ¼-mile zone because of smaller holdings.)

Events of the postwar years presaged the need for protecting the Trail and its environment. Representative Daniel Hoch, an ardent hiker from the Blue Mountain Eagle Climbing Club in Pennsylvania, introduced a bill in 1945 for the National System of Foot Trails as an amendment to the Highway Act. Because it had only a preliminary hearing, it was reintroduced in the next Congress, only to fail again.

But the emphasis was now on preservation of the Trail. It was clear that some kind of help from the Federal Government was essential if an unbroken Trail was to be maintained. In 1964 Senator Gaylord Nelson of Wisconsin introduced a bill to protect and promote the *AT.* Officers of the Conference worked with legislators to draft the bill. Although it did not pass, it demonstrated the strong backing such legislation had from outdoor people generally.

Work continued behind the scenes. In 1968, a broader bill received both strong administration and broad bipartisan support in Congress. The work of years was culminated in its passage.

National Trails System Act

On October 2, 1968, President Johnson signed Public Law 90–543, the National Trails System Act. The Act established a national system of recreation and scenic trails and designated the Appalachian Trail and the Pacific Crest Trail as the first components of the system.

The Act stated that the Appalachian Trail shall be administered primarily as a footpath by the Secretary of the Interior, in consultation with the Secretary of Agriculture. The Secretary was required to establish an Advisory Council of not more than 35 persons to work with the Department on Trail matters.

The law provided for mapping the Trail and publication of its route in the *Federal Register.* Aerial photos were made of the Trail in 1969 and maps indicating the route were published on October 9, 1971 (Vol. 36, No. 197, Part II, pp. 19802–19893).

Following publication in the *Register,* state and local governments were allowed two years to acquire Trail land before Federal action could begin. Then, if these efforts failed, the Federal Government could step in to negotiate rights-of-way or purchase the land directly. Federal purchases by condemnation were provided as a last resort.

The Act *authorized* Federal funds of up to $5 million for the purchase of land for the Appalachian National Scenic Trail. However, the authorization had to be followed by actual *appropriations.* The Federal funds were to come from the Land and Water Conservation Fund.

Despite the promise of the 1968 Act, the process of land acquisition was rather limited through 1976 and 1977. The states acquired less than 100 miles of right of way. The Forest Service of the U.S. Department of Agriculture acquired 156 miles of Trail right of way (and spent about $173,000) within the boundaries of the eight national forests through which the Trail passes. The U.S. Department of the Interior did not acquire any land.

In the spring of 1976, the Secretary of the Interior made $1 million available to states along the Trail which had plans to acquire lands on a matching fund basis. This funding was primarily to be used in Massachusetts, Connecticut, New York, New Jersey, Pennsylvania, and Virginia.

In 1977 two further steps were taken. The first was the initiation of re-survey and mapping of the portion of the *AT* on private land by the National Park Service. Deeds and land records are being examined to determine current ownership of property that borders the Trail. The second step was a revival of interest in the *AT* by the Dept. of the Interior and the Carter administration. At a meeting of the Appalachian Trail Conference in May 1977, Assistant Secretary Robert L. Herbst stated that Interior would promptly begin a land acquisition program and that the department would request Congress to increase the limitation for right of way acquisition from $5 million to $35 million.

This expression of interest was followed by the introduction of bills in Congress in 1977 to amend the National Trails System Act to provide for such funding increases and to make other changes in the law.

—In the House, Rep. Goodloe E. Byron of Maryland sponsored legislation (HR 8803) that would provide for a one-year outlay of $35 million. This proposal was subsequently modified to provide *authorization* for a maximum of $90 million over a three-year period (FY 1978, 1979, and 1980). The proposal also authorized the expansion of the maximum width of the Trail corridor which could be condemned from 200 ft. to 1000 ft., or up to 125 acres per mile rather than 25 acres. The Appalachian National Scenic Trail Advisory Council would be re-established. The amendment was approved by a vote of 409 to 12 on October 26, 1977.

—The Senate version (S 2066) was sponsored by Sen. Charles C. Mathias of Maryland. The Senate, however, ended up acting on the House bill, and proposed a slightly different version. Like the House bill, it provided for *authorization* to spend up to $90 million over a three year period, but the period was changed to FY 1979, 1980, and 1981. Funds not spent in one year could be carried over to the next. The amendment also stated that: "It is the express intent of the Congress that the Secretary should substantially complete the land acquisition program necessary to insure the protection of the Trail within three complete fiscal years following the date of enactment." The Senate amendment was passed by voice vote on February 22, 1978.

The Senate amendment was in turn accepted by the House on March 7, 1978 and was signed by President Carter on March 21, 1978.

Despite the authorization, the annual appropriations fell far short of what was needed to complete the Trail. For 1979 and 1980, $14.6 million and $14.3 million, respectively, were appropriated. Fifty more miles of Trail were bought in 1979, while the preliminary work was finished for acquisition of 644 more parcels.

For 1981, Trail land acquisition was one of the few projects whose appropriation was increased, with $17 million appropriated, but this still fell short of the amount needed. The Administration made an attempt to cut off the 1981 funding, but the funds were restored by Congress.

About $10 million was appropriated for 1982, and 109.7 more Trail miles were brought under protection during that year. Also in 1982, the ATC established the Trust for Appalachian Trail Lands. According to Jim Snow, the purpose of the trust "is to buy lands . . . needed for public conservation and recreation purposes, particularly the right-of-way of the *AT*." The principal objective of the trust "is to protect the land rather than holding or managing it."

According to a recent estimate, $28 million more will be needed to complete protection of the entire Trail. This would make a total of $66 million spent since the 1978 authorization, which would be a very respectable $24 million less than was authorized.

State legislation to protect the Trail is described in the State chapters that follow.

Potomac Appalachian Trail Club

The PATC, founded in November 1927, is one of the 64 organizations that maintain the *AT* under the Conference. It is the third largest in membership (over 3,100 members), surpassed only by the Appalachian Mountain Club in Boston and the Green Mountain Club in Vermont, both older organizations.

Altogether, the PATC is responsible for the maintenance of about 235 miles of the *AT* and about 500 miles of blue-blazed side trails, including trails in Shenandoah National Park, George Washington National Forest, and the Washington, D.C., area. In addition, the PATC built and now maintains the 143-mile Big Blue Trail. The club also operates a network of shelters and cabins.

The PATC issues a number of publications prepared by members. These include the maps and guides cited in Chapter 1 as well as a monthly newsletter, *Potomac Appalachian*. A complete list of publications, with prices, may be obtained from PATC Headquarters.

The PATC has an active Mountaineering Section, which offers assistance and training in rock climbing techniques to beginners, as well as more difficult climbing opportunities for the advanced climber. Information of their weekly activities is contained in *Up Rope,* a monthly publication of the Section, available from the PATC Headquarters. The Club also has a Ski-touring Section and a corresponding newsletter called *Up Slope.*

The Shenandoah Mountain Rescue Group is dedicated to wilderness search and rescue and to outdoor safety. The group meets twice a month at PATC Headquarters and conducts frequent training workshops in the field.

The PATC owns its own headquarters building, which houses its many activities and provides an office to serve the public.

PATC Land Acquisition

Despite the passage of the National Trails System Act, additional efforts are necessary to preserve enough acreage to protect shelters and springs as well as the actual Trail route. Also, with the rapid pace of new commercial developments in the mountains of southern Pennsylvania, Maryland, and northern Virginia, the inevitable delays in procurement of land under the Trails Act may mean the loss of certain areas to the *AT* for good.

In response to this challenge, the PATC established a land acquisition fund in 1968. Since then, a number of parcels and scenic easements have been purchased, mostly in Pennsylvania and Virginia. The club has also received scattered gifts of land and scenic easements. Several splendid cabins have been donated to the club in the last few years. (These are available for member use only.)

Trail Management

Under the National Park Service's management plan for the Appalachian Trail, the burden of responsibility for managing trail land lies with the Appalachian Trail Conference, assisted by local clubs like PATC. With the acquisition program nearly complete in the PATC area, the focus of attention is changing from acquisition to management. PATC is currently setting up various local management committees composed of Club members, local government agencies, adjacent landowners, and National Park Service representatives. In addition, PATC has signed agreements with various National Park Service units and with state agencies in Maryland and Virginia. The most visible role PATC currently plays in land management is "monitoring," the regular inspection of the land to ensure no improper uses (such as logging, dumping or roads) occur.

CHAPTER 3
GEOLOGY ALONG THE TRAIL

During the late Pre-Cambrian and Cambrian eras (800 to 600 million years ago), the area of the Appalachian range was the site of considerable volcanic activity. At least seven distinct lava flows deposited layers of igneous and metamorphic rock (mostly granite and gneiss). The accumulated thickness of this rock was about 1,500 feet.

At the start of the Paleozoic era (600 million years ago), most of the east coast of North America, including the Appalachian area, was covered with large inland seas. Sedimentary layers of clay, sand, and mud filled with lime were deposited. Over a long period of time, the vertical pressure converted these into shale, sandstone, and limestone respectively.

The lateral pressure (from southeast to northwest) created by colliding continental plates caused the uplift of the Appalachian mountains during the late Paleozoic era (about 250 million years ago). In many spots, the once horizontal layers of sedimentary rock were tilted vertically, thus exposing softer rock which then began to erode. The folding, fracturing, and erosion of the crust involved in the uplift resulted in a series of generally parallel ridges. At the same time, the pressures that caused the uplift also changed the nature of many of the rocks. Basalt and sandstone were changed into greenstone and quartz respectively; and more rarely, shale was transformed into slate.

The first uplift exposed what is known as the Summit Peneplain, which includes those flattish mountain peaks and ridges that are usually above 3,500 feet. Two more uplifts, starting in the late Mesozoic era (Cretaceous period, about 135 million years ago), exposed two more erosion levels, known as the Upland and Intermediate Peneplains. The broad, rounded peaks in the Blue Ridge, at about 2,400 to 3,000 feet, belong to the Upland Peneplain; and the spur ridges, foothills, and Blue Ridge of Maryland and northern Virginia, at about 2,300 feet or less, all belong to the Intermediate Peneplain.

The final uplift occurred during the late Tertiary period of the

Cenozoic era (about 7 million years ago), and exposed the Valley-floor, or Shenandoah, Peneplain. This uplift caused the final draining, principally through the Potomac gorge, of an inland sea that had been trapped inside the valley by the Blue Ridge uplift. At earlier times, the Valley had also drained through the present gaps in the Ridge.

South of the Shenandoah National Park boundary, the older, base rock in the center of the Blue Ridge acted as a barrier between the predominantly sedimentary rock of the west and the igneous-metamorphic rock of the east. But north of the Park, the sedimentary zone is farther west, which leaves the Blue Ridge entirely in the igneous-metamorphic zone (except for the area between Bear Pond and the old Shannondale Road). The Blue Ridge Complex rocks, which are the oldest, injection-gneisses that form the core of the Ridge, are exposed only in the area east of the Ridge, in the Upper Piedmont of northern Virginia.

From Harpers Ferry to Bear Pond, granite, granodiorite, augen-gneiss, and granite-gneiss compose the ridge. From Bear Pond to the vicinity of old Shannondale Road, Cambrian sedimentary rocks (500–600 million years old) such as dolomite, limestone, shale, and sandstone compose the Ridge. This explains the presence of such talus slopes as Buzzard Rocks. South to Shenandoah National Park, the Ridge is composed of igneous-metamorphic rocks, from late Pre-Cambrian volcanoes, including schist, slate, phyllite, quartzite, marble, metamorphosed arkose, conglomerite, greenstone, diorite, and gabbro.

In Maryland, the Blue Ridge is composed of Cambrian sediments underlain by basaltic lavas. Lower Cambrian fossils (225–270 million years old) are found in the sediments near the summits, but more than half the strata have been eroded away, exposing the igneous-metamorphic core at the lower elevations. Elk Ridge and South Mountain are both part of the original Blue Ridge formation, while Pleasant Valley resulted from the erosion of soft sediments. The valley between South Mountain and the Catoctin Mountains, however, is a different case, as it was a Triassic basin (inland sea) from 180 million to 225 million years ago.

Worthy of special note are Crescent Rock (Virginia), which is an anticline (upfold), and the Devils Racecourses of Maryland and Virginia, which are alluvial deposits of boulders. These sites dramatically illustrate the tremendous force of their former watercourses.

Because of the nature of the rock, there are no caves in the vicinity of the Trail covered by the *Guide,* except for one at Cavetown, Maryland (which is just northwest of the *AT* crossing of Smithsburg-Wolfsville Road), and possibly an unverified cave mentioned in Maryland Section 3.

There are some copper veins between Raven Rocks and Black Rock, in Maryland. Prospect pits were opened in six places between 1805 and 1865, but all failed because the veins were too small.

No discovery of gems has ever been reported in the area covered by this *Guide.* The semi-precious, cave onyx has been found at Cavetown, Maryland, and jasper is found in the vicinity of Front Royal. The unusual, blue quartz is found at Wevertown.

CHAPTER 4
MARYLAND
GENERAL INFORMATION
Distance 40.67 Miles

The *AT* follows the crest of South Mountain, a name applied to a succession of narrow ridges, from the Pennsylvania line to the Potomac River. Along the river, the Trail is located on the old Chesapeake & Ohio Canal towpath, now part of the Chesapeake & Ohio Canal National Historical Park. From the towpath, the Trail crosses the Potomac on the Goodloe Byron Memorial Footbridge. The continuation of South Mountain across the river, known as Short Hill Mountain, dwindles and becomes indistinguishable among the low foothills of northern Virginia. The Trail is therefore located on a parallel ridge to the west, Blue Ridge Mountain, which forms the boundary between Virginia and West Virginia. Similarly, the extension of Blue Ridge Mountain into Maryland is known as Elk Ridge, which continues north as far as Crampton Gap. Both Elk Ridge and South Mountain are part of the Blue Ridge Mountains of Maryland.

South Mountain is mostly covered with hardwoods and the slopes drain into the tributaries of the Potomac. The numerous views from the Trail include Pen Mar, High Rock, Buzzard Knob, Black Rock Cliffs, Annapolis Rocks, Monument Knob, White Rocks, Crampton Gap, and Weverton Cliffs. South of Monument Knob, the Trail is rich in Civil War history.

In Maryland, the elevation of South Mountain varies from 930 feet, at Crampton Gap, to about 2,000 feet, on the southwest slope of Quirauk Mountain. Lambs Knoll, 1,772 feet, dominates the southern part of the ridge.

The Maryland portion of the Trail has been divided into the following sections:

1. Pen Mar to Raven Rock Hollow .... 6.32 mi.
2. Raven Rock Hollow to Smithsburg-Wolfsville Road .... 3.45 mi.
3. Smithsburg-Wolfsville Road to Interstate 70 .... 8.62 mi.

4. Interstate 70 to Turners Gap.................. 5.04 mi.
5. Turners Gap to Crampton Gap .... 7.22 mi.
6. Crampton Gap to Weverton .... 6.73 mi.
7. Weverton to Harpers Ferry .... 3.29 mi.

Since South Mountain is now a state park along its entire length in Maryland, camping is permitted *only* in designated areas and open fires *only* in fireplaces provided. See list below:

0.3/40.4 Pen Mar County Park (See Shelter/Camping, Section 1, Maryland for exact location.)
5.1/35.5 Devils Racecourse Shelter
9.8/30.8 Hemlock Hill Shelter (no water)
14.6/26.0 Pogo Memorial Primitive Campsite
17.8/22.7 Pine Knob Shelter
21.6/19.0 Washington Monument State Park
23.6/17.0 Dahlgren Camp
25.0/15.6 Rocky Run Shelter (seasonal spring)
30.1/10.5 Crampton Gap Shelter
30.7/9.9 Gathland State Park
38.0/2.5 Weverton Primitive Camp (along C&O Canal, no water)

GROUP CAMPING: Any group of more than ten persons planning to camp in South Mountain State Park should call or write in advance to: Supt. of South Mountain State Park, 900 Arnoldtown Road, Jefferson, Md. 21755. Phone: 301-293-2420.

HISTORY ALONG THE TRAIL

Lack of spectacular scenic grandeur of the Trail in Maryland is compensated for by the significance of its history and its colorful folklore.

Early History

South Mountain served as a barrier that contributed to a pattern of north and south migration by the aborigines. Unlike the open country of the western plains and eastern ridges of the Rocky Mountains, where the edges of open ridges provided the safest travel for the Indians, the crest of South Mountain was not used by the Indians according to tradition. The Indians followed the Monocacy Trail from Pennsylvania, crossing the Potomac at Noland's Ferry. The Monocacy Trail is sometimes called the Warriors Path. On the west side of South Mountain the Delaware Indians in the north and the Catawbas from the south followed the Antietam and Conococheague Creek Valleys, crossing the Potomac at their deltas. Here their battles continued after the arrival of the first white men. In the 1730s and 1740s these valleys became the corridors for German immigrants arriving in the port of Philadelphia bound for the Shenandoah Valley and other parts of Virginia where Lord Fairfax offered inducements for settlement.

A few trappers and settlers crossed South Mountain in the 1720s and 1730s. Israel Friend was mining ore on both sides of the Potomac near the mouth of Antietam Creek in the late 1720s, and a few settlers were farming along Antietam Creek in the early 1730s. By 1732, the Lord Proprietor (Lord Baltimore) caused surveys to be made and began to grant lands on the west side of South Mountain. Comparative safety from the Indians awaited the Treaty of Lancaster in 1744, followed by the purchase of land from the Indians by the Colony of Maryland. The Treaty of Lancaster with the Six Nations permitted the Indians to travel through Maryland from Pennsylvania to the Carolinas and established a temporary boundary between Maryland and Pennsylvania as far west as two miles above the source of the Potomac. For three hundred pounds sterling the Indians provided a quit claim to lands east of this location.

Locations of Early Crossings of South Mountain

The earliest traverse of the South Mountain barrier in Maryland seems to have been through the by-pass along the Potomac, where neutral territory was maintained by the Indian tribes during the spring run of the yellow suckers, and this gap through the Blue Ridge became the earliest thoroughfare of explorers and trappers. Louis Michelle and an exploring party from Annapolis crossed here in 1707. By 1733 Peter Stephens was operating ferries across both the Potomac and Shenandoah Rivers at this gap in the Blue Ridge, and Peter Hoffman, a peddler from Baltimore, was making stops at the Stephens trading post on his route between Frederick and the German settlements in the upper Shenandoah Valley. A foldboat was produced in the government shops at Harpers Ferry and collected by the Lewis and Clark Expedition (1804–1806) at the beginning of their trip for use on western rivers. Later the canal and railroad followed the wagon road when the settlers pushed westward toward the Ohio. Both were in operation in this section by the end of 1834.

The first road to cross the ridge to reach the frontier was "Israel Friend's Mill Road" through Crampton Gap. The crossing through Turners Gap was a foot and horse path until Gen. Braddock's army built a road in 1755 for his wagon train and personal carriage. Passenger stage coach service across the gap was inaugurated on August 1, 1797. Several sessions of the Maryland legislature provided funds for the improvement of the road; in 1806 Turners Gap was designated the route of the National Road, and Federal improvements followed. By the 1850s traffic on the National Road had declined, with the railroads and canal absorbing the freight and passenger traffic.

South Mountain Inn in Turners Gap, which still operates as a tavern (meals and drinks), is one of the oldest public houses along the *AT.* The date of the first tavern in Turners Gap cannot be determined, and the construction of the present building has been estimated as early as 1732 and as late as 1780. It had 22 rooms to rent, and at the height of the traffic on the National Road employed blacksmiths to repair wagons and shoe horses around the clock and kept relay horses in the stables to relieve those exhausted from pulling the steep grade. Abraham Lincoln spent a night at the tavern while on his way to take his seat in Congress, and it was reportedly a favorite hangout of Daniel Webster and Henry Clay. President Jackson, William Henry Harrison, Polk, Taylor and Van Buren passed through Turners Gap when traveling the National Road, and some of them may have stayed overnight in the tavern.

Mrs. Dahlgren, widow of Adm. John A. Dahlgren, commandant of the Washington Navy Yard during the Civil War and credited with perfecting the rifled cannon, bought the tavern in

1876 for a summer home, retaining the name, South Mountain House. She was shocked by the corruption of Christian doctrine among the people of South Mountain. She exposed their "corrupted" beliefs and described their poverty stricken lives in a book published in 1882. For her missionary work among them she built the Gothic stone chapel which overlooks the trail. Restored by Mr. Griffin, 1963–5, the chapel is open on Saturdays, Sundays, and holidays from 1 to 5 p.m.

The Sisters of St. Mary's of Notre Dame used the South Mountain House for a summer retreat from 1922 until 1925, when the property was again sold for commercial purposes. A dancing pavilion was added where the veranda is now located, and at one time "the tavern served as a full-blown brothel." Mitchell H. Dodson purchased the property in 1957. The stucco has been removed from the stone facings, and the original fireplaces have been uncovered.

Mason and Dixon Line

The Mason and Dixon Line, the boundary between Maryland and Pennsylvania, should not be overlooked. During the summer of 1765 Charles Mason and Jeremiah Dixon, British astronomers and surveyors, crossed with a small army of chainbearers, local surveyors, axmen, rodmen, cooks and other laborers. A supporting road westward was constructed to transport supplies and equipment.

The boundary had been in dispute since the grant was made to William Penn in 1681. Lord Baltimore's colonists called the Pennsylvanians "Quaking Cowards", and the latter referred to the Catholics of Maryland as the "Hominy Gentry." The descendents of William Penn and George Calvert, the first Lord Baltimore, agreed to abide by a line which would be surveyed by the two reputable scientists, Mason and Dixon, who were then observing the transit of the planet Venus from a position in Africa. At the time of the survey a line separating slave-holding colonies from the north was not contemplated, although it came to pass that Dixie, or Dixieland, became the name for the area south of the Mason and Dixon Line.

To mark the boundary line between the two colonies, milestones and, at five-mile intervals, crownstones were placed. Milestone No. 91 is the closest to the Appalachian Trail, but it is inaccessibly located on private land in Pen Mar. A nearby crownstone is No. 90, one mile east (as the crow flies), in the village of Highfield. These stones are made of limestone and were transported from England to the land underlaid with limestone.

Industry

Whiskey making was perhaps the first industry along the Trail in Maryland. With the many sources of spring water on the slopes of South Mountain, corn, rye and wheat grown in the valleys were made into whiskey, which was cheaper to ship to market than the bulkier grain. When a Federal tax was placed on whiskey in 1794, the distillers of South Mountain joined their compatriots in western Pennsylvania in "the Whiskey Rebellion." A march on Frederick was organized but disbanded when the rebels learned that 500 Federal troops were waiting for them in Frederick.

Whiskey distilling continued at Smithsburg on the northwest slope of South Mountain and at Burkittsville on the east slope of Crampton Gap into the late 1800s. At Burkittsville in the 1880s the Needwood Distillery (Golden Gate Whiskey) and Ahalt's Distillery were competitors. Both advertised using spring water from South Mountain. For aging and a better flavor J.D. Ahalt shipped his whiskey to Rio de Janeiro and return. Outerbridge Horsey made a better arrangement. After aging in his 3,000-barrel brick warehouse, his Golden Gate whiskey was shipped around the Horn to San Francisco for storage for a year before it was returned to Burkittsville, where it was again aged before sale.

Moonshining along the lower end of South Mountain and adjacent ridges of the Blue Ridge reached an advanced stage during Prohibition, when Spencer Weaver organized the moonshiners into a syndicate for production and marketing. Inducements for moonshiners to join his syndicate included a steady income and "cradle to the grave" fringe benefits.

Moonshiners were paid a monthly salary plus a production incentive based upon a unit price for whiskey delivered. If the occupational hazard of a raid resulted in a jail term for the moonshiner, the salary continued, and loans for capital equipment, repayable from later production proceeds, were made available for the re-establishment of the moonshiner in business.

Weaver provided a widow's pension in the event of an accidental death of the moonshiner, and he also had a standing arrangement with a funeral home in Harpers Ferry to cover burial costs. Spencer Weaver used the former "Salty Dog Saloon" across the Potomac from Harpers Ferry for a control center for his operations. But prosperity may have ruined Weaver; he started drinking his own product and mild heart attacks followed. One night he backed his auto into the C&O Canal and was found dead.

Iron making became an important industry near South Mountain where there were trees to burn for charcoal. The Frederick Forge of the 1750s became the Antietam Ironworks after Washington County was formed from Frederick in 1776. Catoctin Furnace was located to the north and east, Mount Aetna to the north and west, Keep Tryst near Harpers Ferry, and the Blue Ridge Ironworks at Knoxville. The installations at Harpers Ferry were heavy consumers of charcoal.

The effect of the iron furnaces on South Mountain were twofold. First, they provided employment for charcoal burners on South Mountain, and second, the denuding of the slopes by burning the hardwoods for charcoal caused erosion and contributed to the floods of the Potomac in the 19th century. A tannery, which operated for approximately 100 years at Burkittsville, also contributed to the erosion by buying tanbark stripped from chestnut and oak trees. Some of the charcoal burners remained behind on the mountain, eking out a meager existence into the 20th century.

Weverton was an unsuccessful industrial town despite its natural advantages. Casper W. Wever, after a successful career as a highway and railroad construction engineer, used his savings to purchase land and water rights and construct industrial buildings to found the town of Weverton. Wever favored the railroad over the canal and opposed a right-of-way through his property for the canal company. (When most of his buildings lay idle he refused to lease space for a temporary hospital for canal workers who contracted Asiatic cholera in the epidemic of 1833.) Wever believed that the drop of 15 feet in the Potomac above Weverton was sufficient to provide water power to turn 300,000 textile spindles (one source estimated 600,000). In 1834 he started construction on industrial buildings for leasing, and a diagonal dam across the Potomac for diverting water into his millrace to provide power for the buildings.

It was reported that Wever's lease charges were too high and the buildings were not constructed to meet the specifications of small factories. Only two buildings were leased, one for marble cutting, and the other by a company that made files for the national armory in Harpers Ferry. The Weverton enterprise failed before the Civil War.

The springs at Weverton have always been important to the community. Scharf refers to a hotel at Weverton built in 1796, which burned before 1880, and which was one of the first hotels in the country to offer rooms with running water for ladies and gentlemen. The replacement hotel built in 1880 also had running water. The sons of the last owner, Harry G. Traver, remember that the water was piped from the spring down the hill to the hotel, and that the water was used to cool beer and watermelon in the hotel, which then catered to railroad workers. The hotel site was where Md-67 connected with US-340 before the 1964–65 relocation. The hotel was razed for the road construction in 1916.

Weverton has been without industry since the Trail was built, and even the railroad station where steam locomotives puffed on the siding while taking on water was dismantled during World War II.

The Chesapeake and Ohio Canal is now a historical park administered by the National Park Service. Intersecting the Appalachian Trail, it provides a comparatively level path along the Potomac for 184.5 miles from Washington to Cumberland.

Operation came to an end in 1924 when a flood damaged its structures. It had operated at a loss for many years, and the low traffic did not warrant sizable new capital expenditures for repairs and improvements.

Civil War and the Memorial Arch to War Correspondents

More words have been devoted to South Mountain in the Civil War than to any other subject along the *AT* in Maryland. In addition, metal tablets in Turners and Crampton Gaps provide details on troop movements during the Battle of South Mountain.

Briefly, the Battle of South Mountain, September 14, 1862, was the curtain raiser for the Battle of Antietam or Sharpsburg. Finding lost Orders No. 191 revealed to the Union Command General Lee's orders to split his army into four segments and the routes for the three task forces detailed to capture Harpers Ferry, by-passed by the Confederates in the northern invasion. Union forces, superior in number and equipment, moved slowly and met strong resistance from small Confederate holding forces entrenched where the *AT* crosses Turners, Fox, Crampton and Brownsville Gaps.

The Confederate command post was in the South Mountain Inn at Turners Gap. The delay permitted the three task forces under Stonewall Jackson to capture Harpers Ferry and permitted the Confederates to regroup on the west side of Antietam Creek, where the two armies fought each other to a stand-still. Three days of fighting beginning on South Mountain resulted in the highest casualty rate of the war.

A Civil War correspondent, George Alfred Townsend, returned to South Mountain after the war, and in 1884, flush with the proceeds from his books of fiction and syndicated newspaper articles on the Washington scene (he was the Drew Pearson of the post-Civil War period), he bought Crampton Gap and constructed a home, a house for his wife, a hall, a library, a lodge, a guest house, servants' houses, stables and a tomb for himself, where he was not buried. He called his estate "Gathland," "Gath" being his nom de plume. The buildings, mostly constructed of stone, have been vandalized and only a wing of Gath Hall has been restored. The arch, dedicated in 1896 as a memorial to Civil War correspondents and artists, survives intact.

The 50-foot high memorial dominates Crampton Gap and frames the Catoctin Valley. It faces toward two other battlefields, Gettysburg and Winchester. The arch contains many inscriptions, and mythological figures are recessed in the stonework.

The off-balance arch has been described as an architectural cross between a Moorish arch and the tower on an old Frederick fire company station. The Hagerstown version is that Townsend adapted his architecture from the front of the Antietam Fire Co. building across from the B&O R.R. Station (now demolished for a parking lot) in Hagerstown, where Townsend observed the off-balance arch while awaiting transportation to his estate.

The arch is under the administration of the National Park Service, while the surrounding 135-acre park, Gathland State Park, is administered by the Maryland Department of Natural Resources. The Governor of Maryland, in rededicating the State Park in 1960, called for the establishment of a National Newspaper Hall of Fame in a building to be constructed north of the arch, where outstanding newsmen of the past 100 years from all the States of the Union would be commemorated.

Monument to George Washington

The first monument to George Washington to be completed is on Monument Knob north of Turners Gap. The observatory, 30 feet high and constructed of native stone, is shaped like an old fashioned cream bottle. Here gathered citizens from Boonsboro on July 4, 1827, "to spend the day at hard labor. An aged survivor of the Revolution delivered an address and at its conclusion a cold collation was spread," according to an early reporter. The people of the South Mountain area like ceremonies, and this monument and the one in Crampton Gap have been rededicated several times. Restored by the CCC in 1934–35, the monument is included in the Washington Monument State Park with picnicking and camping facilities.

Monument to George Washington

Resorts

A few resorts flourished along the Appalachian Trail in Maryland. The first Black Rock Hotel, believed to have been built shortly after the Civil War, burned in 1880, and after rebuilding in 1907, the occupancy period was short. South Mountain Inn in Turners Gap advertised itself as a summer resort from 1852 to 1859 after the drop in traffic on the National Road.

The popularity of Pen Mar near the Pennsylvania line more than compensated for the lackluster of other resorts. At the turn of the century the area supported seven hotels and about 100 boarding houses. A Lutheran picnic drew 15,000 to Pen Mar Park, and 5,000 was not uncommon on a summer day when it was known as the Coney Island of the Blue Ridge. Special trains with several sections were scheduled by the Western Maryland R.R. from both east and west. Families were encouraged to spend the summer at Pen Mar while the breadwinners commuted to Baltimore, Hagerstown, and Waynesboro, which was connected with Pen Mar by trolley. The Blue Mountain House, a rambling three-story, frame structure, accommodating 400 overnight guests, featured 50-cent Sunday dinners. It was built in 1883 and burned in 1913.

The Western Maryland R.R. opened Pen Mar Park in 1878 to promote passenger traffic and supplement railway income. Promotional publicity for the park claimed the observatory on High Rock could hold 500 people on its three tiers. The amusement park was leased to other operators in 1928 when the railroad management found that nine out of ten patrons of the park came by auto and bus. Pen Mar Park continued to operate with declining business until gas rationing in 1943 forced it to close.

History of the Appalachian Trail in Maryland

The first trail use along the crest of South Mountain may have been as a route for fugitive slaves making their way north, a link in the Underground Railway. Five of John Brown's men made their way north along South Mountain after the abortive raid on Harpers Ferry. Among John Brown's effects were maps showing mountain forts, and some believe that his strategy may have included building crude forts along South Mountain to cover their retreat after the raid.

A continuous trail along the ridge was not in evidence when the Appalachian Trail was laid out and built across Maryland by members of the PATC. The Trail was marked, cleared and paint-blazed in the winter of 1931 and spring of 1932.

The five open shelters on South Mountain were constructed in the 1938–41 period. Bear Spring Cabin was dedicated by the PATC on May 1, 1941. Members of the Mountain Club of Maryland, located in Baltimore, and the Maryland Appalachian Trail Club of Hagerstown assisted members of the PATC in locating sites and negotiating leases with the owners. The Civilian Conservation Corps provided labor and the PATC supplied materials and technical assistance in the construction.

The preservation of the *AT* is now the main problem facing the Clubs in this area. Summer homes and other buildings are beginning to encroach on the Trail.

Maryland's Department of Forests and Parks in the mid 1950s announced a plan to acquire land on South Mountain for watershed protection, including the practice of forestry and recreation. By 1964 approximately 4,000 acres had been acquired. The plan lay dormant during the ensuing five years with the exception of the development of the Greenbrier Park. Frederick County, during this period, classified most of the east slope in private ownership in a recreational category which bars new homes for permanent residences but excludes land uses existing at the time of rezoning.

In May 1970, Maryland became the second state to pass legislation to protect the Appalachian Trail. The Bill (S.84) directed the State to acquire land, for the purpose of protecting and maintaining the Trail across the State. The Bill was introduced by State Senator Goodloe Byron of Frederick in January 1970, and was signed by Governor Mandel on May 5, 1970. The *AT* is currently included in the South Mountain State Park. Land acquisition, now under Program Open Space of the Department of Natural Resources, is moving ahead.

Although the proposed amendments to the National Trails

System Act discussed in Chapter 2 were introduced by two Maryland legislators (Rep. Goodloe E. Byron and Sen. Charles C. Mathias), Maryland does not presently plan to apply for any Federal funds. It expects to complete its purchases solely with state open space funds.

SELECTED REFERENCES

For a complete footnoted version of the preceding history, see the sixth edition. The following publications are among the principal sources:

Dahlgren, Madeline V., *South Mountain Magic,* Boston, James R. Osgood, 1882. Reprinted 1974, Washington Co. Public Library, Hagerstown, Md.

Maryland Geological Survey, *Report on the Highways of Maryland,* Baltimore, Johns Hopkins University Press, 1889.

Maryland Geological Survey, *Report on the Resurvey of the Maryland-Pennsylvania Boundary,* Baltimore, 1908.

Salzberg, Michael, "Boonsboro Washington Monument," *Washington Post,* March 5, 1970.

Sanderlin, Walter S., *The Great National Project, A History of the Chesapeake and Ohio Canal,* Baltimore, Johns Hopkins University Press, 1946.

Scharf, Thomas J., *A History of Western Maryland,* Philadelphia, Louis H. Everts, 1882.

Schletterbeck, Judy, *The Pen Mar Story,* 1977 (privately published).

Williams, Thomas, J.C., *A History of Washington County, Maryland,* Hagerstown, Runk and Titsworth, 1906, Vol. 1.

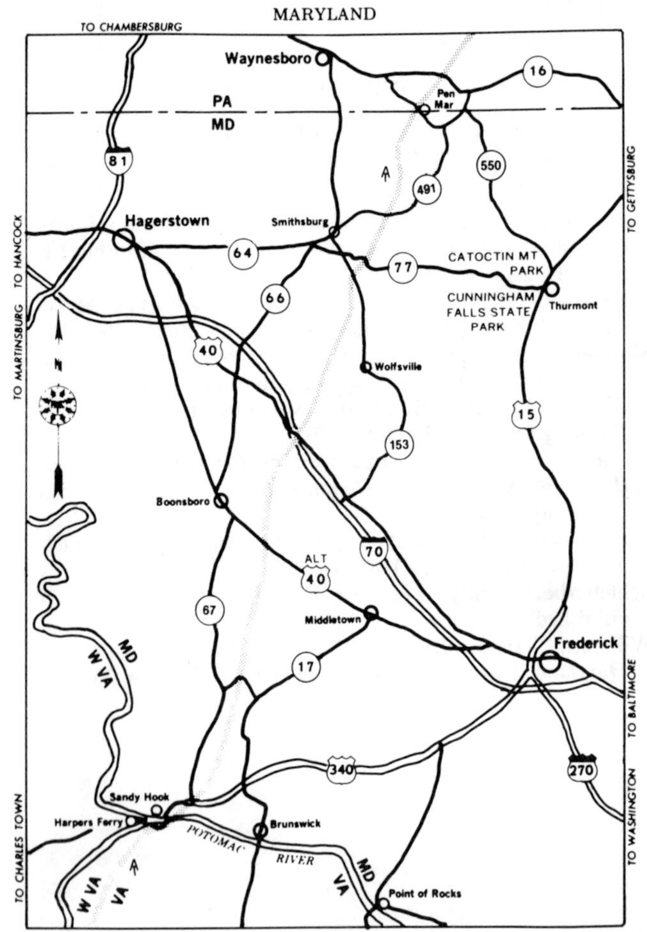
MARYLAND
TO CHAMBERSBURG
Waynesboro
16
Pen Mar
PA
MD
81
550
491
TO GETTYSBURG
TO HANCOCK
Hagerstown
Smithsburg
64
77
CATOCTIN MT PARK
66
CUNNINGHAM FALLS STATE PARK
Thurmont
TO MARTINSBURG
40
Wolfsville
15
153
Boonsboro
70
ALT 40
67
Middletown
Frederick
MD
W VA
17
TO BALTIMORE
340
270
TO WASHINGTON
Sandy Hook
TO CHARLES TOWN
Harpers Ferry
Brunswick
POTOMAC
RIVER
MD
VA
W VA
VA
Point of Rocks

SECTION 1
PEN MAR TO RAVEN ROCK HOLLOW
Distance 6.32 Miles

Road Approaches and Parking

To reach Pen Mar: From US-15, take Md-550 (Sabillasville Road) west. Turn right at entrance to Ft. Ritchie, staying on Md-550. Shortly after, turn left and pass under trestle. A sign at this turn says "Pen Mar Park." Turn right onto Pen Mar Road. (To reach Pen Mar County Park, continue straight ahead.) Cross into Pennsylvania and over railroad tracks. The *AT*, going south, follows the powerline right-of-way on left. There is room for two cars to park on the right side of the gate here. Do not block gate! Distance is 71 miles from Washington, D.C.

From I-81, take Md-16 east. Turn right onto Md-418 and left onto Pen Mar Road. The *AT*, going south, follows the powerline right-of-way on right just before bridge over railroad tracks. See above. Distance is 4 miles from Waynesboro.

To reach Raven Rock Hollow: From I-70, take Md-66 north. Turn right onto Md-64 and right onto Md-491 (Raven Rock Road). *AT*, going north, ascends from stop-sign at intersection with Ft. Ritchie Road (sign says "Camp Ritchie Road"), on left. There is room for four cars to park on the shoulders of Ft. Ritchie Road. Distance is 2.8 miles from Smithsburg.

From US-15, take Md-77 west. Turn right onto Md-64, then see above.

Points of Interest

Pen Mar County Park (at 0.34/5.98 mi.) has an outstanding westward view. A former resort, established by the Western Maryland Railroad, was in operation on this site between 1877 and 1943. Vestiges of former habitation can be seen just south of the park. High Rock (at 3.03/3.20 mi.) offers an excellent westward view and is a popular site for hang-gliding. Devils Racecourse (0.36 mi. down the Devils Racecourse Shelter Trail, at 5.22/1.10 mi.) is an ancient stream deposit of boulders. Raven Rock, an unusual outcrop, is visible from Md-491 between autumn and spring.

Maps

PATC Map #5 and USGS Smithsburg Quadrangle

Shelter/Camping

Devils Racecourse Shelter (0.27 mi. down the Devils Racecourse Shelter Trail, at 5.22/1.10 mi.) accommodates seven persons and has a *spring* nearby. It is also accessible from Ft. Ritchie Road (see chapter on "Side Trails").

Free camping is allowed in a designated location in Pen Mar County Park (at 0.34/5.98 mi.). Follow the paved promenade 0.12 mi. through the park to High Rock Road. Camping is permitted in the two fields bounded by High Rock Road, Chestnut St., Pennsylvania Ave., and Walnut St. Saturday-night campers must leave by 9 a.m. Sunday morning. No public water is available November through April. During these months, it is advisable to call 301–791–3125 during working hours. Camping is *prohibited* except at the above locations. Open fires are allowed only where fireplaces are provided.

Supplies

Water is available at Pen Mar County Park (May through October) and Devils Racecourse Shelter. The Park also has a telephone.

Brief Description

The ascent of Quirauk Mountain from the north is the most strenuous on the *AT* in Maryland, while from the south it is somewhat easier. The main points of interest are concentrated in the northern half of this section.

North to south: The *AT* first passes, with little change in elevation, through Pen Mar County Park and a formerly inhabited forest. Then the Trail becomes increasingly rough, turns abruptly eastward, and ascends very steeply by switchbacks and over rocks. After passing closely to High Rock, the Trail continues to ascend steeply on an old road. Upon reaching the highest elevation (just over 2,000 feet) for the *AT* in Maryland, the Trail turns southward and descends gradually on old roads along the ridge crest. The Trail descends the eastern side of the ridge very steeply from a saddle just north of Raven Rock knoll.

South to north: The *AT* ascends the eastern side of the ridge very steeply and reaches the crest at a saddle just north of Raven Rock knoll. Then the Trail ascends gradually on old roads along the ridge crest. Upon reaching the highest elevation (just over 2,000 feet) for the *AT* in Maryland, the Trail turns westward and descends steeply on an old road. After passing closely to High Rock, the Trail descends very steeply over rocks and by switchbacks. At the foot of the cliff, the Trail turns abruptly northward. The footing becomes good again as the Trail passes, with little change in elevation, through a formerly inhabited forest and Pen Mar County Park.

Side Trails

High Rock loop (at 3.03/3.29 mi. and 3.12/3.20 mi.)
Devils Racecourse Shelter Trail (at 5.22/1.10 mi.)

Detailed Trail Data—North to South

0—Pen Mar Road. Follow powerline right-of-way (an old trolley line).

0.04—View down powerline corridor on right. Go straight.

0.07—Turn left onto intersecting path, ascend, and cross railroad tracks.

0.13—Turn right onto gravel road that ascends parallel to the railroad tracks. Cross gate ahead.

0.34—Pen Mar County Park. Outstanding westward view. *Water,* rest rooms, pay phone in Visitors Interpretive Center (open May-October), and parking area are to left. Though there is no entrance fee, the parking area is gated. Open 9 a.m. to sunset all year. *Camping is permitted at the designated location* (see above, under "Shelter/Camping"). Bear right, crossing paved walkways, pass between two pavilions, and follow level gravel road ahead.

0.61—Turn left off road and ascend path, crossing embankment. *This is very easy to miss.*

0.63—Turn right onto old road that parallels the previous one. Trail is level through forest of maple and chestnut oak.

1.01—Turn left at junction.

1.04—Turn right off road and onto path.

1.08—Faint road on right leads, in a few yards, to the brick-lined cellar of a former house. A stone-lined root-cellar is next to it. Many vestiges of former habitation may be seen in the forest ahead.

1.16—Large mound on left, with stone retaining wall, old wire fence, and metal moorings, encloses a large pit. This was probably an artificial pond at one time.

1.26—Cross stone retaining wall and turn right onto old road.

1.30—Cross telephone line.

1.46—Cross old road. Collapsed ruin of house on left corner. Trail becomes rocky in open forest ahead. *Follow blazes carefully.*

1.66—Cross old road and descend ahead.

2.54—Turn sharply left at large boulder and ascend very steeply.

2.64—Narrow, well-engineered switchbacks begin.

2.73—End of switchbacks, but continue steeply over rocks. *Watch for poison ivy.*

2.94—Level.

3.03—*AT* goes right at fork. (Left trail is also blazed white and leads to High Rock on a 0.23 mi. loop, which rejoins the *AT* 0.09 mi. ahead. High Rock has a spectacular view and is a popular hang-gliding site. Ruins of a former pavilion [stone columns and a wooden platform] stand on the rock. The ungated, but narrow, paved High Rock Road leads directly down to Pen Mar County Park. There is plenty of room to park at High Rock.)

3.12—Turn right onto old road at junction and ascend. White-blazed High Rock loop rejoins on left.

3.20—Descend.

3.45—Ascend steeply.

3.68—Highest elevation (just over 2,000 feet) for the *AT* in Maryland. The Trail turns southward and descends through denser undergrowth.

3.94—Go right at fork.

4.58—Beautiful open forest begins. The Trail passes a few hemlocks ahead, an unusual growth on a ridge crest.

5.22—Blue-blazed Devils Racecourse Shelter Trail intersects on left. It leads to shelter and *spring* in 0.27 mi. and to Ft. Ritchie Road in 0.42 mi.

5.31—Go left onto path at fork.

5.58—Edge of cliff with winter view to east. Turn right and descend on switchbacks. Treacherous when wet or when leaves are down.

5.89—Come into level, old road, then descend through hemlocks ahead.

6.32—Intersection of Md-491 and Ft. Ritchie Road (sign says "Camp Ritchie Road") in Raven Rock Hollow. (Raven Rock, an unusual jutting cliff, is on the north side of Md-491. It can be seen, between autumn and spring, by walking a short distance to the right on Md-491.) To continue on the Trail, cross Md-491.

Detailed Trail Data—South to North

0—From the stop-sign at the intersection of Md-491 and Ft. Ritchie Road (sign says "Camp Ritchie Road"), in Raven Rock Hollow, the *AT* ascends through hemlocks on an old road. (Raven Rock, an unusual jutting cliff, is on the north side of Md-491. It can be seen, between autumn and spring, by walking a short distance to the left on Md-491.)

0.43—Ascend on switchbacks. Climb cliff just ahead and bear right along its top edge. Treacherous when wet or when leaves are down.

0.74—Winter view to east. Turn left, away from cliff, and ascend gradually.

1.01—Bear right onto old road at junction.

1.10—Blue-blazed Devils Racecourse Shelter Trail intersects on right. (It leads to shelter and *spring* in 0.27 mi. and to Ft. Ritchie Road in 0.42 mi.) Ahead, the Trail passes through a beautiful open forest containing a few hemlocks, an unusual growth on a ridge crest.

1.74—Open forest ends as undergrowth becomes denser.

2.38—Bear left at junction, staying on road that follows ridge crest.

2.64—Highest elevation (just over 2,000 feet) for the *AT* in Maryland. The Trail turns westward and descends steeply through lighter undergrowth.

2.87—Ascend.

3.12—Descend.

3.20—Turn left off road at junction. (White-blazed High Rock loop [0.23 mi. long] leads straight ahead on road, passes High Rock, and rejoins the *AT* 0.09 mi. ahead. High Rock has a spectacular view and is a popular hang-gliding site. Ruins of a former pavilion [stone columns and a wooden platform] stand on the rock. The ungated, narrow, paved High Rock Road leads directly down to Pen Mar County Park. There is plenty of room to park at High Rock.)

3.29—High Rock loop rejoins on right. Go straight.

3.38—Descend steeply over rocks. *Watch for poison ivy.*

3.59—Narrow, well-engineered switchbacks begin.

3.68—End of switchbacks, but continue to descend very steeply over rocks in open forest. *Follow blazes carefully.*

3.78—Turn sharply right at large boulder and ascend.

4.66—Cross old road. Trail is generally level ahead.

4.86—Cross old road. Footing improves ahead as the Trail follows an old road. Collapsed ruin of house on right corner.

5.02—Cross telephone line.

5.06—Turn left off road and cross stone retaining wall.

5.16—Large mound on right, with stone retaining wall, old wire fence, and metal moorings, encloses a large pit. This was probably an artificial pond at one time. Many vestiges of former habitation may be seen in this vicinity.

5.24—Faint road on left leads, in a few yards, to the brick-lined cellar of a former house. A stone-lined root-cellar is next to it.

5.28—Turn left onto road at junction.

5.31—Turn right onto intersecting road and pass through forest of maple and chestnut oak.

5.69—Turn left onto path and descend. *This is very easy to miss.*

5.71—Turn right onto road that parallels the previous one.

5.98—Pen Mar County Park. Outstanding westward view. *Water,* rest rooms, pay phone in Visitors Interpretive Center (open May–October), and parking area are to right. Though there is no entrance fee, the parking area is gated. Open 9 a.m.

to sunset, all year. *Camping is permitted at the designated location* (see above, under "Shelter/Camping"). Cross paved walkways, bear left, and descend on gravel road.

6.19—Turn left at junction, cross railroad tracks, and descend on path.

6.25—Turn right and follow powerline right-of-way (an old trolley line).

6.28—View down powerline corridor on left. Go straight.

6.32—Pen Mar Road. To continue on the Trail, cross road and follow powerline right-of-way.

SECTION 2
RAVEN ROCK HOLLOW
TO SMITHSBURG-WOLFSVILLE ROAD
Distance 3.45 Miles

Road Approaches and Parking

To reach Raven Rock Hollow: From I-70, take Md-66 north. Turn right onto Md-64 and right onto Md-491 (Raven Rock Road). The *AT,* going south, descends to right, opposite intersection with Ft. Ritchie Road (sign says "Camp Ritchie Road"). There is room for four cars to park on the shoulders of Ft. Ritchie Road. Distance is 2.8 miles from Smithsburg.

From US-15, take Md-77 west. Turn right onto Md-64, then see above.

Warner Gap Road: This gravel road leads one mile east from Md-491 to the *AT,* which crosses the road at the edge of a farm on the left. There is room for two cars to park on the shoulder *but watch for poison ivy.* Distance is 2.7 miles from Smithsburg.

Foxville Road (Md-77): There is no parking where this road crosses the *AT.* Distances are 2.3 miles west to Smithsburg, 2.7 miles east to Foxville, and 8.7 miles east to Thurmont.

To reach Smithsburg-Wolfsville Road (Md-153): From the east, on I-70, take the Myersville exit. Turn right onto Wolfsville Road (Md-153) in the center of Myersville. After passing through Wolfsville, this becomes the Smithsburg-Wolfsville Road. The *AT,* going north, follows a nameless gravel road, which intersects Md-153 at a point 0.4 miles north of the intersection with Garfield Road and Loy-Wolfe Road. There is room for three cars to park beside Md-153, and room for two cars beside the nameless gravel road, near its junction with Md-153. Smithsburg is 2 miles northwest, Wolfsville is 3.75 miles south, and Washington, D.C., is 69.4 miles away.

From the west, on I-70, take Md-66 north. Turn right onto Md-64. Then turn right onto Md-153 and see above.

Points of Interest

The jagged rocks of Buzzard Knob (0.15 mi. up a side trail, at 0.50/2.95 mi.) offer a mediocre view, and a high-tension power-line right-of-way offers a spectacular view (at 2.58/0.87 mi.).

Maps

PATC Map #5 and USGS Smithsburg Quadrangle

Supplies

Water is available from a *spring* at 0.85/2.60 mi.

Camping

Camping and open fires are prohibited in this section.

Brief Description

This section is geographically interesting in that it crosses two small ridges that form a curious, right-angle interruption in the South Mountain range. These ridges extend southeastward and link with the Catoctin range. The excellent footing will come as a relief after either adjoining section, but the extremely steep hill at the powerline will be very hard on backpackers going either direction.

North to south: Between two tributaries of Little Antietam Creek, from Raven Rock Hollow to Warner Gap Hollow, the Trail passes over a saddle east of Buzzard Knob. Then the Trail climbs over another small ridge, crosses Md-77, and drops into a deep ravine (Grove Creek). After climbing out of the ravine, the Trail follows a powerline right-of-way and a gravel road to the Smithsburg-Wolfsville Road.

South to north: From the Smithsburg-Wolfsville Road, the Trail follows a gravel road and a powerline right-of-way. Then it drops into a deep ravine (Grove Creek). After climbing out of the ravine, the Trail crosses Md-77 and climbs over a small ridge. Between two tributaries of Little Antietam Creek, from Warner Gap Hollow to Raven Rock Hollow, the Trail passes over a saddle east of Buzzard Knob.

Side Trails

To Buzzard Knob (at 0.50/2.95 mi.)

Detailed Trail Data—North to South

0—From Md-491, descend embankment and cross Little Antietam Creek through a relatively young hemlock grove. (The hemlocks in this area were lumbered in 1941.) Then cross telephone line and ascend.

0.14—Go right at fork onto a recent relocation. Just ahead, the Trail passes a large hole and some short, vertical, metal pipes, which are probably remnants of the former lumbering operation. Then the Trail turns left and ascends steeply through a dense hemlock grove, passing another hole, which is on the right.

0.37—Cross large stone wall.

0.44—Turn right at junction at end of relocation.

0.50—Top of saddle. A few yards ahead, a blue-blazed trail leads right 0.15 mi. to two mediocre views (to WSW and to N) from the jagged peak of Buzzard Knob. The trail is very steep and requires a rock scramble. *Be careful of loose rocks.*

0.63—Old road intersects on left. Go straight and descend steeply.

0.80—Turn left onto Warner Gap Road. In 35 yards, turn right, off the road, and cross Little Antietam Creek. *Don't take water from this creek.* This is a relocation that is not correctly shown on the PATC map.

0.85—Bear to right of stone wall. There is a *spring* beside the Trail, under the hemlocks on the right. Ascend very steeply on the right side of the ravine (not the left, as shown on the PATC map).

1.07—Cross old road and ascend gradually.

1.11—Bear right onto old road at junction.

1.17—Cross high-tension powerline. No view.

1.30—Turn right onto old road at junction.

NOTE: A major relocation is being planned for remainder of this section.

1.70—Old road intersects on left. Go straight. Level.

1.78—Pass house on left and cross old road. *Stay on Trail.*

1.85—Old road intersects on left. Go straight.

1.99—Old road intersects on left. Go straight and pass house on right.

2.13—Private driveway intersects on left. Bear right and descend between a trailer and a house.

2.19—Cross Md-77 (Foxville Road), bearing to right of Gun

Club entrance, and descend very steeply ahead. This is a recent relocation to avoid the Gun Club.

2.26—Pass under an impressive outcrop of overhanging rocks.

2.37—Cross polluted tributary of Grove Creek and ascend very steeply with rocky footing.

2.58—Leave woods at intersection of high-tension powerline and underground cable right-of-ways. Spectacular view here. Bear left and ascend on the far side of extremely steep, grassy hill of the cable right-of-way. Cross to opposite side of clearing at top of hill.

2.69—End of relocation. The old *AT* route (going N), still highly visible, entered the woods here. Turn right and follow the cable right-of-way, which soon rejoins the powerline corridor.

3.03—The Trail crosses a dirt road, and then comes into a dirt road that crosses the powerline corridor.

3.12—The road becomes graveled as it comes out of the woods onto private land beside a house. *Stay on road.* Just ahead, descend past a rare, large, healthy American chestnut, in yard on right.

3.45—Smithsburg-Wolfsville Road (Md-153). To continue on the Trail, cross the road.

Detailed Trail Data—South to North

NOTE: A major relocation is being planned from this point to mile 2.15.

0—From Smithsburg-Wolfsville Road (Md-153), follow nameless gravel road. It descends at first, then ascends. *Stay on road.*

0.28—Pass a rare, large, healthy American chestnut, in private yard on left. Just ahead, the gravel ends as the road enters woods.

0.42—Cross high-tension powerline, turn left, and cross dirt road. The Trail follows the powerline right-of-way on the north side, then follows an underground cable right-of-way, which angles away from the powerline.

0.76—Cross to opposite side of clearing and descend extremely steep, grassy hill. (The old *AT* route, still highly visible, enters the woods here, but it should no longer be followed.) Bear right at the bottom of the hill, where the cable and powerline corridors intersect, and cross back to the north side of the clearing. Spectacular view all along here.

0.87—Enter woods and descend very steeply with rocky footing.

1.08—Cross polluted tributary of Grove Creek and ascend very steeply.

1.19—Pass under an impressive outcrop of overhanging rocks.

1.26—Cross Md-77 (Foxville Road) and ascend driveway between trailer and house.

1.32—Go left at fork. (The "No Trespassing" sign applies only to the right fork.) Level. *Stay on Trail.*

1.46—Old road intersects on right. Go straight and pass house on left.

1.60—Old road intersects on right. Go straight.

1.67—Cross old road and pass house on right.

1.75—Old road intersects on right. Go straight and descend.

2.15—Turn left onto intersecting old road.

2.28—Cross high-tension powerline. No view.

2.34—Go left at fork.

2.38—Cross old road and descend very steeply on the left side of the ravine (not the right, as shown on the PATC map, which does not include this recent relocation).

2.60—There is a *spring*, under the hemlocks on the left, beside the Trail. Just ahead, cross Little Antietam Creek (*don't take water from creek*) and turn left onto Warner Gap Road.

2.65—After 35 yards on Warner Gap Road, turn right off road and ascend steeply.

2.82—Old road intersects on right. Go straight and ascend more gradually.

2.95—Top of saddle. A few yards before, a blue-blazed trail leads left 0.15 mi. to two mediocre views (to WSW and to N) from the jagged peak of Buzzard Knob. The trail is very steep and requires a rock scramble. *Be careful of loose rocks.*

3.01—Go left at fork onto a recent relocation and descend steeply.

3.08—Cross large stone wall. The Trail passes through a dense growth of young hemlocks ahead. (The hemlocks in this area were lumbered in 1941.) The Trail also passes two large holes and some short, vertical, metal pipes, which are probably remnants of the former lumbering operation.

3.31—Old *AT* route intersects on right at end of relocation. Go straight and descend, crossing a telephone line and Little Antietam Creek. Then ascend embankment.

3.45—Md-491, in Raven Rock Hollow. To continue on the Trail, cross Md-491 to the stop-sign at the intersection of Ft. Ritchie Road (sign says "Camp Ritchie Road").

Black Rock Cliffs

SECTION 3
SMITHSBURG-WOLFSVILLE ROAD TO INTERSTATE 70
Distance 8.62 Miles

Road Approaches and Parking

To reach Smithsburg-Wolfsville Road (Md-153): From the east, on I-70, take the Myersville exit. Turn right onto Wolfsville Road (Md-153) in the center of Myersville. After passing through Wolfsville, this becomes the Smithsburg-Wolfsville Road. The *AT*, going south, ascends a gullied road that is opposite a nameless gravel road at a point 0.4 miles north of the junction of Md-153, Garfield Road, and Loy-Wolfe Road. There is room for three cars to park beside Md-153, and room for two cars beside the nameless gravel road, near its junction with Md-153. Smithsburg is 2 miles northwest, Wolfsville is 3.75 miles south, and Washington, D.C., is 69.4 miles away.

From the west, on I-70, take Md-66 north. Turn right onto Md-64. Then turn right onto Md-153 and see above.

To reach the Interstate 70 crossing: From the east, on I-70, take the Myersville exit. Turn right onto Wolfsville Road (Md-153) in the center of Myersville, then turn left onto US-40. There is room for about 20 cars to park at two pullovers just before US-40 crosses over I-70. From the parking area, cross the embankment and follow the closed section of old highway. At end of old highway, take path around left side of guard rail. Then bear sharply left and descend steeply to footbridge over I-70, on right. (Distance is 0.13 mi. from parking.) Turn right onto dirt road between fence and hillside for northbound *AT*; or go straight over footbridge for southbound *AT*. Distance is 60 miles from Washington, D.C.

From the west, on I-70, take the US-40 exit south, just outside of Hagerstown. Cross I-70 overpass and park at pullover on right immediately after. Then see above. Distance is 10 miles from Hagerstown.

Points of Interest

Black Rock Cliffs (at 5.41/3.21 mi.) and Annapolis Rocks (0.20 mi. down a side trail, at 6.41/2.21 mi.) offer outstanding westward views. A talus slope (at 2.11/6.51 mi.) offers a good eastward view. The Black Rock Springs Hotel site (0.26 mi. down a side trail, at 4.89/3.73 mi.) is of historical interest.

Maps

PATC Map #5 and USGS Smithsburg and Myersville Quadrangles

Shelters and Campgrounds

Hemlock Hill Shelter and the surrounding campground (at 0.08/8.54 mi.) are privately owned and maintained by Alfred Henneberger, and their use is free on a first-come, first-served basis. It accommodates six persons. *There is no source of water.* Fires are allowed only within the cement fire-rings.

Pine Knob Shelter (0.14 mi. down a side trail, at 8.16/0.46 mi.) accommodates five persons and has a *spring* nearby.

The Pogo Memorial Primitive Campsite (0.26 mi. down a side trail, at 4.89/3.73 mi.) was established by the Mountain Club of Maryland as a memorial to their late member, Walter "Pogo" Rheinheimer, Jr. (1958–1974). Intended for *AT* thru-hikers only, its use is free, on a first-come, first-served basis. The campground has a privy and a nearby *spring. The location shown on PATC Map #5 is wrong;* see "Detailed Trail Data."

Camping and open fires are permitted *only* in the locations described above.

Public Accommodations

A restaurant and phone are opposite the entrance to Greenbrier State Park, 0.5 mi. west of the US-40 parking area. A privy and a display map are at the US-40 parking area.

Supplies

Water is available from *springs* near Black Rock Springs Hotel site (0.30 mi. down a side trail, at 4.89/3.73 mi.), Annapolis Rocks (0.20 mi. down a side trail, at 6.41/2.21 mi.), and Pine Knob Shelter (0.14 mi. down a side trail, at 8.16/0.46 mi.).

Brief Description

This section presents a typical example of the narrow ridge crest peculiar to Maryland. The Trail follows old roads except for two rough stretches along the crest. The southern half is easier and has the main points of interest. The predominant growth is oak and hickory.

North to south: The *AT* ascends the eastern side of the ridge very steeply and then crosses to the western side, where it follows a generally level route just below the rocky crest. This is succeeded by two rough segments where the Trail follows the crest. (The second of these is a recent relocation that detours the Hotel site.) After briefly descending to the headwaters of Black Rock Creek, the Trail climbs past Black Rock Cliffs and Annapolis Rocks, cliffs with excellent westward views. Then the Trail descends gradually, ascends briefly at Pine Knob, and drops steeply thereafter.

South to north: The *AT* climbs steeply to Pine Knob, descends briefly, and then ascends gradually past Annapolis Rocks and Black Rock Cliffs, cliffs with excellent westward views. After descending to the headwaters of Black Rock Creek, the Trail detours the Hotel site by a rough, new relocation along the crest. Next the Trail follows an old road over a smoother portion of the crest, but this is succeeded by a segment where the crest becomes rocky again. After descending slightly to the western side of the crest, the Trail follows an old road that parallels the crest. Then the Trail crosses to the eastern side and descends very steeply.

Side Trails

To Pogo Memorial Primitive Campsite and Black Rock Springs Hotel site (at 4.89/3.73 mi.)

To Black Rock Cliffs (at 5.41/3.21 mi.)

To Annapolis Rocks (at 6.41/2.21 mi.)

To Pine Knob Shelter (at 8.16/0.46 mi.)

Detailed Trail Data—North to South

0—Smithsburg-Wolfsville Road (Md-153). Ascend steeply on gullied road, which is still used for logging.

0.08—Pass through Hemlock Hill campground. Shelter on right. *No water.* Ascend more steeply ahead.

0.36—Generally level ahead.

0.65—Turn right at junction and ascend very steeply.

0.78—Cross ridge crest and descend to western side. Go left at fork just ahead. Then the generally level Trail parallels the rocky crest, which offers many eastward winter-views.

1.94—Leave road and make short ascent to rocky crest, where the Trail is very rough. There was a small sawmill near here when this area was lumbered 40 years ago.

2.11—Good eastward view from talus slope on left.

2.29—End of worst rocks. *Watch for poison ivy.* Trail becomes a slightly undulating old road ahead.

2.92—Footing improves.

3.36—Pass old road that intersects on right.

3.63—Go right at fork.

3.69—Descend.

3.84—Bear right at junction with old road. To left, this road descends steeply to junction of Loy Wolfe Road and Black Rock Road in 0.9 mi., as shown on PATC Map #5. This makes possible, for hikers who can follow the unblazed route, two circuit hikes using the Loy Wolfe Road, a very pleasant country road. (Straight ahead, an abandoned trail leads to cliffs with an eastward view, in 0.12 mi. via right fork, and to caves via left fork. Though not visible in summer, this may be of interest to experienced bushwhackers in winter.)

3.94—Old road (leading to Jugtown) intersects on right. Go straight.

4.02—Turn left off road and onto path. This recent relocation, a detour of the Black Rock Springs Hotel site and the Pogo Memorial Campsite, is *easy to miss.* (The old route, which passes both sites and a *spring,* is 0.32 mi. shorter than the relocation. To follow it, descend straight ahead on the blue-blazed road. Go left at two successive forks and intersect the old Bagtown Road in 0.29 mi. To right, blazes lead to *spring* in 70 yards, where they end. Straight ahead, blazes lead to *AT* in 0.26 mi. Black Rock Springs Hotel site and Pogo Memorial Campsite are on hillside to left.)

4.09—Ascend steeply with rocky footing.

4.19—Level ridge crest.

4.69—Descend steeply with rocky footing through open forest.

4.89—End of relocation. Bear left onto old road, cross intermittent Black Rock Creek, and ascend. To right, blue-blazed road leads to Hotel site and Pogo Memorial Campsite (see above).

5.41—Blue-blazed trail on right leads a short distance to Black Rock Cliffs. This 180-degree westward view is the best in this section. Note the considerable scree at the foot of the cliff.

5.77—Level.

6.41—Blue-blazed trail on right leads 0.20 mi. to Annapolis Rocks, an overhanging cliff with an excellent westward view that includes Greenbrier Lake. A *spring* is to the south. Descend gradually ahead, with many level sections.

6.85—Old road intersects on left. Bear right.

7.42—Ascend steeply.

7.56—Go left around island, then go straight past old road that intersects on left.

7.68—Level crest, just slightly below Pine Knob. Pass old road that intersects on right.

7.76—Go right at fork. Descend very steeply past laurel.

7.97—Pass old road that intersects on right. Descend less steeply. Go right around island just ahead.

8.06—Go left at fork. Just ahead, stay on road and pass two paths that intersect on right.

8.16—Blue-blazed trail on right leads 0.14 mi. to Pine Knob Shelter and *spring*. There are also numerous good campsites near the shelter.

8.22—Cross telephone line.

8.40—Pass road leading to farmhouse on left. Then turn right onto intersecting road just ahead.

8.52—Pass under US-40 overpass. Continue ahead on dirt road parallelling I-70.

8.62—Footbridge over I-70. To continue on the Trail, turn right and cross footbridge. (To reach parking area, privy, restaurant, and phone on US-40, turn left up hillside, then turn left again and ascend trail to abandoned section of highway. Follow old highway to parking area and privy. Distance is 0.13 mi. Restaurant and phone are 0.5 mi. west on US-40.)

Detailed Trail Data—South to North

0—Footbridge over I-70. Turn left onto dirt road that passes between fence on left and hillside on right. (To reach parking area, privy, restaurant, and phone on US-40, go straight up hillside, then turn left and ascend trail to abandoned section of highway. Follow old highway to parking area and privy. Distance is 0.13 mi. Restaurant and phone are 0.5 mi. west on US-40.)

0.10—Pass under US-40 overpass. Just ahead, dirt road ascends to right and into woods.

0.22—Turn left at junction. Just ahead, pass road leading to farmhouse on right.

0.40—Cross telephone line.

0.46—Go right at fork. Blue-blazed trail leads left 0.14 mi. to Pine Knob Shelter and *spring*. There are also numerous good campsites near the shelter. Just ahead, stay on the road and pass two paths that intersect on left.

0.56—Bear right at junction with old road. Go left around island just ahead.

0.65—Go right at fork and ascend steeply past laurel.

0.86—Level crest, just slightly below Pine Knob. Pass old road that intersects on right.

0.94—Pass old road that intersects on left and descend steeply.

1.06—Go right around island, then go straight past old road that intersects on right.

1.20—Trail ascends gradually ahead, with many level sections.

1.77—Go left at fork.

2.21—Blue-blazed trail on left leads 0.20 mi. to Annapolis Rocks, an overhanging cliff with an excellent westward view that includes Greenbrier Lake. There is a *spring* slightly to the south. Level ahead.

2.85—Descend.

3.21—Blue-blazed trail on left leads a short distance to Black Rock Cliffs. This 180-degree westward view is the best in this section. Note the considerable scree at the foot of the cliff.

3.73—Cross intermittent Black Rock Creek, immediately bear right off road, and ascend steeply with rocky footing. This recent relocation, a detour of the Black Rock Springs Hotel site and the Pogo Memorial Campsite, is *easy to miss*. (The old route, which passes both sites and a *spring*, is 0.32 mi. shorter than the relocation. To follow it, continue ahead on the blue-blazed road. Reach junction with old Bagtown Road (on left) in 0.26 mi. Pogo Memorial Campsite and Hotel site are on hillside on right. Blazes continue down Bagtown Road, ending at *spring* in 70 yards. To continue on former *AT* route, ascend blue-blazed road from junction with Bagtown Road. Pass two old roads that intersect on left and rejoin *AT* in 0.29 mi. from Bagtown Road junction.)

3.93—Level ridge crest.

4.43—Descend steeply with rocky footing.

4.53—Level.

4.60—Turn right onto old road at junction. End of relocation.

4.68—Old road (leading to Jugtown) intersects on left. Go straight and ascend ahead.

4.78—Go left at fork. To right, road descends steeply to junction of Loy Wolfe Road and Black Rock Road in 0.9 mi., as shown on PATC Map #5. This makes possible, for hikers who can follow an unblazed route, two circuit hikes using the Loy Wolfe Road, a very pleasant country road. (To right of fork, an abandoned trail leads to cliffs with an eastward view, in 0.12 mi. via right fork, and to caves via left fork. Though not visible in summer, this may be of interest to experienced bushwhackers in winter.)

4.99—Old road intersects on right. Bear left.

5.26—Go right at fork.

5.70—Rocky footing. Trail undulates ahead.

6.33—*Watch for poison ivy,* after road becomes path. Rocky crest just ahead.

6.51—Good eastward view from talus slope on right. Just ahead, descend to western side of crest.

6.68—Trail becomes a road again. There was a small sawmill near here when this area was lumbered 40 years ago. Ahead, the generally level Trail parallels the crest, which offers many eastward views in winter.

7.84—Old road intersects on left. Bear right and cross to eastern side of crest. Then descend very steeply.

7.97—Turn left onto intersecting road, which is still used for logging. Generally level ahead.

8.26—Descend very steeply.

8.54—Pass through Hemlock Hill campground. Shelter on left. *No water.* Descend less steeply.

8.62—Smithsburg-Wolfsville Road (Md-153). To continue on the Trail, cross Md-153 and follow nameless gravel road.

Annapolis Rocks

SECTION 4
INTERSTATE 70 TO TURNERS GAP
Distance 5.04 Miles

Road Approaches and Parking

To reach the Interstate 70 crossing: From the east, on I-70, take the Myersville exit. Turn right onto Wolfsville Road (Md-153) in the center of Myersville, then turn left onto US-40. There is room for about 20 cars to park at two pullovers just before US-40 crosses I-70. From the parking area, cross the embankment and follow the closed section of old highway. At the end of old highway, take path around left side of guard rail. Bear sharply left and descend steeply to footbridge over I-70, on right. Distance is 0.13 mi. from parking; 60 miles from Washington, D.C.

From the west, on I-70, take the US-40 exit south, just outside of Hagerstown. Cross I-70 overpass and park at pullover on right immediately after. Then see above. Distance is 10 miles from Hagerstown.

To reach Turners Gap: From the east, on I-70, take US-Alt. 40 west. The *AT*, going north, follows Dahlgren Road on the right at Turners Gap. There is no dependable parking in the vicinity, but the owners of Old South Mountain Inn (0.1 mi. west of *AT*) often allow day-hikers to park for free, behind the inn, if permission is asked. Distance is 57 miles from Washington, D.C.

From the west, US-Alt. 40 diverges from US-40 just outside of Hagerstown, but has no junction with I-70. US-Alt. 40 may also be reached, from I-81, via Md-68; or from Shepherdstown, via Md-34. Then see above. Distance is 2 miles from Boonsboro.

From US-340, take Md-67 north and turn right onto US-Alt. 40. Then see above.

To reach Washington Monument State Park: From US-Alt. 40 at Turners Gap, turn north onto Monument Road. Cross Zittlestown Road and enter park. Entrance and parking are free, but the gate is locked at night. Open 8:00 a.m. to 9:30 p.m. in season; 10:00 a.m. to sunset in off-season. Season is from April through October.

Points of Interest

The first monument ever erected to George Washington (at 2.95/2.09 mi.), in Washington Monument State Park, offers a spectacular westward view. Dahlgren Road offers an excellent southward view (at 4.56/0.48 mi.). At Turners Gap, the Old South Mountain Inn and Dahlgren Chapel are of historical interest. Also, part of the Battle of South Mountain was fought in the vicinity of Turners Gap.

Maps

PATC Map #5 and #6, and USGS Myersville and Middletown Quadrangles

Campground

Washington Monument State Park allows camping only at designated sites during season (April through October). There are *no overnight shelters.* (Picnic shelters for day use only.) Nightly fee per person is $1.50 for *AT* backpackers; for others, $3.00 for Maryland residents, $4.00 for non-residents, and half-price for citizens 62 or older. Use of sites is on a first-come, first-served basis, or by reservation (write to Superintendent, Washington Monument State Park, Route 1, Middletown, MD). *Camping and fires are prohibited everywhere else in this section.*

Public Accommodations

Old South Mountain Inn (at Turners Gap) provides dinner 5 p.m.–9 p.m. Tuesday through Friday; Saturday noon–10 p.m. and Sunday brunch at 10:30 a.m.–2 p.m., regular meals to 8 p.m. No lodging.

Supplies

Boonsboro (2 miles west of Turners Gap) has grocery and hardware stores and a post office.

Water is available at Washington Monument State Park (at 3.07/1.97 mi.). The Park also has a telephone.

Brief Description

This very easy section crosses a succession of low hills almost entirely on forest roads.

North to south: After crossing I-70 on a footbridge, the *AT* climbs over the small Bartman Hill. Then the Trail undulates along a low ridge culminating in a short, steep ascent of Monument Knob, in Washington Monument State Park, where it passes the first monument to George Washington. After leaving the park, the Trail briefly follows a paved road, and then crosses another low hill, which has a profuse growth of poison ivy. Descending through a major focus of heavy fighting during the Battle of South Mountain, the Trail reaches the graveled Dahlgren Road, which is followed to Turners Gap.

South to north: From Turners Gap, the *AT* ascends through a major focus of heavy fighting during the Battle of South Mountain as it follows the graveled Dahlgren Road and an old forest road (which has a profuse growth of poison ivy). Then the Trail briefly follows a paved road into Washington Monument State Park and makes a short, steep ascent of Monument Knob, where it passes the first monument to George Washington. After leaving the park, the Trail undulates along a low ridge, climbs over the small Bartman Hill, and crosses I–70 on a footbridge.

Detailed Trail Data—North to South

0—Cross footbridge over I–70.

0.06—End of bridge. Ascend, turn left and go up stairs, and then turn right and walk on easement between two houses. *Stay on Trail.*

0.11—Cross paved Boonsboro Mountain Road and ascend Bartman Hill on old dirt road. Pass through hickory, oak, maple, dogwood and sassafras.

0.50—Descend.

0.71—Old road intersects on right. Go straight.

0.78—Cross paved Old Wolfsville Road and ascend ahead.

0.85—Cross telephone line.

0.96—Go right at fork off road and onto path.

1.07—Descend through lots of laurel, chestnut oak, and American chestnut shoots.

1.20—Level.

1.31—Cross dirt road.

1.39—Go left onto dirt road at junction.

1.45—Old road intersects on left. Go straight and ascend.

2.12—Unmarked path leads left short distance to rocks with good winter view. Level, then descend steeply.

2.48—Level.

2.64—Cross high-tension powerline and ascend Monument Knob very steeply with rocky footing.

2.83—Large talus slope with good view on right. *Be careful of loose rocks.*

2.91—Intersect graveled path. Go straight up hill.

2.95—Pass first monument to George Washington. (First built in 1827, and restored by CCC in 1934–36. See "History Along the Trail.") Interior stairs lead to a spectacular view from top of monument. Descend very steeply on graveled path ahead.

3.07—Parking lot for Washington Monument State Park. Rest rooms and water fountain are downhill to right. No camping is permitted within park, except at designated sites (see above, under "Campground"). Turn left and descend paved road. Just ahead, turn right off road and into woods.

3.27—Cross campground road.

3.33—Turn right onto paved road again and pass park gate just ahead.

3.37—Cross Zittlestown Road and ascend straight ahead on Monument Road, passing houses and fields.

3.49—Turn left off road and into maple-dominated woods just before hill crest. This is private land. *Stay on Trail.* Ahead, the Trail passes through an extremely profuse growth of *poison ivy.* (The area ahead was the scene of heavy fighting during the Battle of South Mountain, Sept. 14, 1862. The Federal right flank, under Hooker, enveloped the Confederate left flank, under Rodes, with Dahlgren Road as the attack's focal point.)

NOTE: The Trail will soon be relocated between here and Turners Gap.

3.75—Descend and pass through stone fence ahead.

3.81—Pass through stone fence and ascend.

3.94—Path on right leads short distance to small cliff with winter view. Level.

4.12—Descend.

4.42—Pass through fence.

4.56—Turn right onto graveled Dahlgren Road. Splendid 180-degree view from this junction. Lambs Knoll (with fire-tower) is visible.

5.04—US-Alt. 40 at Turners Gap. (To right 0.1 mi. is Old South Mountain Inn, used by several Presidents. At least 200 years old, it is one of the oldest public houses along the *AT.* Opposite the inn is a Gothic stone chapel (open Saturdays, Sundays, and holidays, 1–5 p.m.) built by the widow of Admiral Dahlgren, inventor of the Dahlgren cannon.) To continue on the Trail, cross US-Alt. 40.

Detailed Trail Data—South to North

0—US-Alt. 40 at Turners Gap. Ascend graveled Dahlgren Road. (To left 0.1 mi. is Old South Mountain Inn, used by several Presidents. At least 200 years old, it is one of the oldest public houses along the *AT.* Opposite the inn is a Gothic stone chapel (open Saturdays, Sundays, and holidays, 1–5 p.m.) built by the widow of Admiral Dahlgren, inventor of the Dahlgren cannon.)

NOTE: The Trail will soon be relocated between here and Monument Road.

0.48—Turn left onto dirt road with fence on each side. Splendid 180-degree view from this junction. Lambs Knoll (with fire-tower) is visible. The Trail crosses private land ahead. *Stay on Trail.* (This junction and the Trail just ahead were the scene of heavy fighting during the Battle of South Mountain, Sept. 14, 1862. The Federal right flank, under Hooker, enveloped the Confederate left flank, under Rodes, with Dahlgren Road as the attack's focal point.)

0.62—Pass through fence. In the woods ahead, the Trail passes through an extremely profuse growth of *poison ivy.*

0.92—Level.

1.10—Path on left leads short distance to small cliff with winter view. Descend.

1.23—Pass through stone fence and ascend.

1.27—Pass through stone fence and descend just ahead through abundant maple.

1.55—Turn right onto paved Monument Road. Pass houses and open fields ahead.

1.67—Cross Zittlestown Road.

1.71—Turn left off road and onto path shortly after passing entrance gate for Washington Monument State Park. No camping is permitted within park, except at designated sites (see above, under "Campground"). Ascend.

1.77—Cross campground road.

1.94—Turn left onto paved road.

1.97—Parking lot. Rest rooms and water fountain are downhill to left. Turn right and ascend very steeply on graveled path.

2.09—Pass first monument to George Washington. (First built in 1827, and restored by CCC in 1934–36. See "History Along the Trail.") Interior stairs lead to spectacular view from top of monument. Continue ahead on graveled path.

2.13—Go straight, leaving graveled path, at curve. Descend very steeply.

2.21—Large talus slope with good view on left. *Be careful of loose rocks.*

2.40—Cross high-tension powerline. Level.

2.56—Ascend steeply ahead.

2.92—Unmarked path leads right short distance to rocks with good winter view. Descend ahead.

3.59—Old road intersects on right. Go straight. Level.

3.65—Go right off road and onto path at fork.

3.73—Cross dirt road.

3.84—Ascend through lots of laurel, chestnut oaks, and American chestnut shoots.

3.97—Descend.

4.08—Bear left onto intersecting old road.

4.19—Cross telephone line.

4.26—Cross paved Old Wolfsville Road and ascend Bartman Hill.

4.33—Old road intersects on left. Go straight.

4.54—Descend through hickory, oak, maple, dogwood, and sassafras.

4.93—Cross paved Boonsboro Mountain Road and follow easement between two houses. *Stay on Trail.* Then turn left, descend stairs, turn right, and cross footbridge over I-70.

5.04—End of footbridge. To continue on the Trail, turn left and follow dirt road.

Pleasant Valley

SECTION 5
TURNERS GAP TO CRAMPTON GAP
Distance 7.22 Miles

Road Approaches and Parking

To reach Turners Gap: From the east, on I-70, take US-Alt. 40 west. The *AT,* going south, follows an old dirt road opposite Dahlgren Road. There is no dependable parking in the vicinity, but the owners of Old South Mountain Inn (0.1 mi. west of *AT*) often allow dayhikers to park for free, behind the inn, if permission is asked. (On weekends, park cars in Park, using one car space at the inn for shuttle.) Distance is 57 miles from Washington, D.C.

From the west, US-Alt. 40 diverges from US-40 just outside of Hagerstown, but has no junction with I-70. US-Alt. 40 may also be reached, from I-81, via Md-68; or from Shepherdstown, via Md-34. Then see above. Distance is 2 miles from Boonsboro.

From US-340, take Md-67 north and turn right onto US-Alt. 40. Then see above.

Reno Monument Road: There is no parking at this *AT* crossing.

To reach Crampton Gap: From US-Alt. 40 (see above), take Md-67 south (from west), or Md-17 south (from east). Then turn onto Gapland Road (Md-572), which leads to a free parking lot in Gathland State Park at Crampton Gap. Distance is 59.2 miles from Washington, D.C., and 1.2 miles from the center of Burkittsville.

From US-340, take Md-67 north (from west), or Md-17 north (from east), and see above.

Points of Interest

At Turners Gap, the Old South Mountain Inn and Dahlgren Chapel are of historical interest. Part of the Battle of South Mountain was fought in the vicinity of Turners Gap, but heavier fighting centered around Fox Gap, where a monument to Major General Reno may be seen (0.23 mi. east on Reno Monument Road, at 0.83/6.39 mi.). The small quartzite cliff known as White Rocks (0.06 mi. by side trail, at 3.74/3.48 mi.) offers a southward view that is poor in summer, but excellent in winter. At Crampton Gap, scene of another Civil War battle, a memorial to Civil War correspondents and the ruins of Gathland may be seen.

Maps

PATC Map #6 and USGS Middletown and Keedysville Quadrangles

Shelters and Campground

Dahlgren Backpack Camping Area (at 0.24/6.98 mi.), established and maintained by the Maryland Park Service, has numerous excellent sites, rest rooms, *water,* and *showers.* Use is free on a first-come, first-served basis.

Rocky Run Shelter (0.22 mi. by side trail, at 1.66/5.56 mi.), first built by the CCC in 1940–41, accommodates five persons. Seasonal spring.

Crampton Gap Shelter (0.25 mi. by side trail, at 6.81/0.41 mi.), first built by the CCC in 1941, accommodates eight persons. *Water* at Park.

Bear Spring Cabin (0.70 mi. by side trail, at 4.26/2.96 mi.) is a locked cabin owned by the PATC. See under "Use of the Guide and the Trail."

Camping is permitted at above camping areas only.

Public Accommodations

Old South Mountain Inn (at Turners Gap) provides meals, but not lodging. (See Section 4: *Public Accommodations.*)

Supplies

Boonsboro (2 miles west of Turners Gap) has grocery and hardware stores and a post office.

Water is available at Dahlgren Backpack Camping Area (at 0.24/6.98), from *Bear Spring* (0.32 mi. by side trail, at 4.26/2.96 mi.), and at Crampton Gap.

Brief Description

This is a relatively easy section with generally excellent footing. The ascent of Lambs Knoll is steeper from the north.

North to south: From Turners Gap, the *AT* crosses the ridge and passes to the west of Fox Gap, the scene of heavy fighting during the Battle of South Mountain. Then the Trail follows a steep, S-shaped route to the summit of Lambs Knoll, a peculiar offset in the ridge. After a short descent of the escarpment, the Trail descends gradually along a narrow ridge similar to Sections 3 and 6 to reach Crampton Gap.

South to north: From Crampton Gap, the *AT* ascends gradually along a narrow ridge similar to Sections 3 and 6. After a short ascent of the escarpment, the Trail passes the summit of Lambs Knoll, a peculiar offset in the ridge. Then the Trail steeply descends an S-shaped route to the west of Fox Gap, the scene of heavy fighting during the Battle of South Mountain. The Trail then crosses the ridge to reach Turners Gap.

Side Trails

To Rocky Run Shelter (at 1.66/5.56 mi.)
White Rocks Trail (at 3.74/3.48 mi.)
Bear Spring Cabin Trail (at 4.26/2.96 mi.)
To Crampton Gap Shelter (at 6.81/0.41 mi.)

Detailed Trail Data—North to South

0—US-Alt. 40 at Turners Gap. Descend old road opposite Dahlgren Road. Trail is level just ahead. (To right 0.1 mi. is Old South Mountain Inn, used by several Presidents. At least 200 years old, it is one of the oldest public houses along the *AT.* Opposite the inn is a Gothic stone chapel (open Saturdays, Sundays, and holidays, 1–5 p.m.) built by the widow of Admiral Dahlgren, inventor of the Dahlgren cannon.)

0.05—Turn left at junction with dirt road. No camping here.

0.10—Turn left off road.

0.24—Pass Dahlgren Backpack Camping Area on right. *Water,* rest rooms, and showers. Just ahead, ascend on old road past profuse dogwood.

0.61—Bear right off road and onto path. Descend with rocky footing.

0.74—Cross old trail. Forest ahead is almost entirely chestnut oak.

0.83—Cross paved Reno Monument Road, west of Fox Gap (originally "Fox's Gap"), which was the scene of heavy fighting during the Battle of South Mountain, Sept. 14, 1862. (The Federal left flank, under Reno, enveloped the Confederate right flank, under Garland, and later under Hood, with the gap as the attack's focal point. Major General Jesse L. Reno and Brigadier General Samuel Garland were killed in the battle, and Rutherford B. Hayes, a future President, was wounded.) Reno Monument, erected by veterans of the 9th U.S. Army Corps on Sept. 14, 1889, is a steep 0.23 mi. to left.

0.88—Ascend.

1.19—Cross high-tension powerline. Excellent westward view.

1.37—Turn right onto old road. Level.

1.66—Go left at fork and ascend very steeply. Blue-blazed trail leads right 0.22 mi. to Rocky Run Shelter.

NOTE: The Trail will soon be relocated between here and Lambs Knoll.

1.96—Cross old road.

2.11—Cross paved road. (Road leads right to summit of Lambs Knoll; left to Reno Monument Road.)

3.49—Summit of Lambs Knoll (1,772 feet). Profuse laurel. (Former Maryland Forest Service Reno Firetower and a government installation are both on the right. The tower is closed and should not be climbed. The area is posted "No Trespassing.") Descend.

3.74—Blue-blazed White Rocks Trail leads left 0.06 mi. to a poor summer view, but excellent winter view. See chapter on "Side Trails."

3.81—Go right at fork onto recent relocation and descend ahead. Azaleas, red maples, and chestnut shoots here.

4.06—Pass rock outcrop on left.

4.08—End of relocation. Pass old *AT* route, which intersects on left.

4.26—Turn right at junction. Blue-blazed Bear Spring Cabin Trail leads left 0.32 mi. to *Bear Spring* and 0.70 mi. to locked cabin. See chapter on "Side Trails." Ahead, the Trail undulates with rocky footing through forest with dense undergrowth.

4.90—Winter view on left. Descend gradually.

5.10—Small view of Elk Ridge and Pleasant Valley from large rockpile on right. Footing improves.

5.55—Very interesting knoll, on left, which exhibits an evenly fractured pile of boulders. An excellent winter viewpoint.

6.81—Blue-blazed trail leads left 0.25 mi. to Crampton Gap Shelter.

6.93—Go right at fork off road and onto path.

7.12—Trail rejoins old road.

7.15—Gathland State Park, in Crampton Gap (originally "Crampton's Gap"). The park has *water,* rest rooms, phone, and a museum. Camping is prohibited, except at designated sites (see under "Campground," Maryland Section 6). Pass field, picnic tables, and ruins of large stone barn (circa 1887). Heavy fighting occurred here during the Battle of Crampton's Gap, Sept. 14, 1862. (The Federals, under Franklin, eventually overwhelmed the greatly outnumbered Confederates, under McLaws.)

7.22—Pass through gap in stone fence and reach Gapland Road (Md–572). (To the left are historical markers and a stone memorial to Civil War newspaper correspondents, erected by George Alfred Townsend, a Civil War journalist who used the pen-name "Gath." On the hill ahead is Gath Hall, of the Townsend estate, which was restored as a museum in 1958.) To continue on the Trail, cross Md–572 and ascend paved road straight ahead.

Detailed Trail Data—South to North

0—Gapland Road (Md–572), in Gathland State Park, at Crampton Gap (originally "Crampton's Gap"). The park has *water,* rest rooms, phone, and a museum. Camping and fires are prohibited, except at designated sites (see under "Campground," Maryland Section 6). (To the right are historical markers and a stone memorial to Civil War correspondents, erected by George Alfred Townsend, a Civil War journalist who used the pen-name "Gath." On the hill to the south is Gath Hall, of the Townsend estate, which was restored as a museum in 1958.) Pass through gap in stone fence and cross field. Heavy fighting occurred here during the Battle of Crampton's Gap, Sept. 14, 1862. (The Federals, under Franklin, eventually overwhelmed the greatly outnumbered Confederates, under McLaws.)

0.07—Pass ruins of large stone barn (circa 1887) and picnic tables. Ascend old road.

0.10—Go left at fork off road and onto path.

0.29—Trail rejoins old road.

0.41—Blue-blazed trail leads right 0.25 mi. to Crampton Gap Shelter.

1.67—Very interesting knoll, on right, exhibits an evenly fractured pile of boulders. An excellent winter viewpoint.

2.12—Small view of Elk Ridge and Pleasant Valley from large rockpile on left. Footing becomes rocky.

2.32—Winter view on right. Trail undulates ahead through forest with dense undergrowth.

2.96—Turn left onto intersecting trail and ascend. Blue-blazed Bear Spring Cabin Trail leads straight 0.32 mi. to *Bear Spring* and 0.70 mi. to locked cabin. See chapter on "Side Trails."

3.14—Go straight onto recent relocation at fork.

3.16—Pass rock outcrop on right.

3.41—End of relocation. Turn left at junction. Azaleas, red maples, and chestnut shoots here.

3.48—Blue-blazed White Rocks Trail leads right 0.06 mi. to a poor summer view, but an excellent winter view. Profuse laurel ahead.

3.73—Summit of Lambs Knoll (1,772 feet). (Former Maryland Forest Service Reno Firetower and a government installation are both on the left. The tower is closed and should not be climbed. The area is posted "No Trespassing.") Descend steeply ahead.

NOTE: The Trail will soon be relocated between here and Rocky Run Shelter.

5.11—Cross paved road. (Road leads left to summit of Lambs Knoll, right to Reno Monument Road.) Take right-hand, old, dirt road and descend very steeply.

5.26—Cross old road.

5.56—Bear right at junction. Blue-blazed trail leads left 0.22 mi. to Rocky Run Shelter. Level ahead.

5.85—Turn left onto intersecting old road and descend.

6.03—Cross high-tension powerline. Excellent westward view.

6.34—Ascend.

6.39—Cross paved Reno Monument Road, west of Fox Gap (originally "Fox's Gap"), which was the scene of heavy fighting during the Battle of South Mountain, Sept. 14, 1862. (The Federal left flank, under Reno, enveloped the Confederate right flank, under Garland, and later under Hood, with the gap as the attack's focal point. Major General Jesse L. Reno and Brigadier General Samuel Garland were killed in the battle, and Rutherford B. Hayes, a future President, was wounded.) Reno Monument, erected by the veterans of the 9th U.S. Army Corps on Sept. 14, 1889, is a steep 0.23 mi. to right. Rocky footing ahead through forest that is almost entirely chestnut oaks.

6.48—Cross old trail.

6.61—Bear left onto old road and descend through profuse dogwood.

6.98—Pass Dahlgren Backpack Camping Area on left. *Water,* rest rooms, and showers.

7.12—Turn right onto dirt road.

7.17—Turn right onto dirt road. No camping here.

7.22—US-Alt. 40 at Turners Gap. (To left 0.1 mi. is Old South Mountain Inn, used by several Presidents. At least 200 years old, it is one of the oldest public-houses along the *AT.* Opposite the inn is a Gothic stone chapel (open Saturdays, Sundays, and holidays, 1-5 p.m.) built by the widow of Admiral Dahlgren, inventor of the Dahlgren cannon.) To continue on the Trail, cross US-Alt. 40 and ascend Dahlgren Road.

NOTE: The Trail will soon be relocated between here and Monument Road.

Memorial Arch, Gathland State Park

SECTION 6
CRAMPTON GAP TO WEVERTON
Distance 6.73 Miles

Road Approaches and Parking

To reach Crampton Gap: From US–Alt. 40, take Md–67 south (from west), or Md–17 south (from east). Then turn onto Gapland Road (Md–572), which leads to a free parking lot in Gathland State Park, at Crampton Gap. Distance is 59.2 miles from Washington, D.C., and 1.2 miles from the center of Burkittsville.

From US–340, take Md–67 north (from west), or Md–17 north (from east), and see above.

Brownsville Pass Road: On Md–67, park at picnic area beside nameless access road to Brownsville. Overnight parking is not recommended. Hike access road into Brownsville and turn left onto nameless main street of town. Then turn right onto paved road identified by a sign as "Brownsville Pass." This ascends and becomes a dirt road after the last house. Some old blazes are still visible in the woods. Distance from picnic area to Brownsville Gap is about one mile. Distance from Brownsville to Weverton is 4.4 miles.

To reach Weverton: From US–340, take Md–67 north. Then take first right, turning onto nameless road. There is lots of room to park on right, in clearing beside abandoned section of old highway, at curve in road. The *AT,* going north, follows the nameless road toward the ridge. Distance is 61 miles from Washington, D.C.

From US–Alt. 40, take Md–67 south. Then take the last left turn, onto nameless road, before reaching the US–340 junction. Then see above.

Points of Interest

Crampton Gap, scene of heavy fighting during the Civil War, has preserved earthworks, a memorial to Civil War newspaper correspondents, a museum, and the ruins of Gathland. At several places along the ridge, rocky knolls exhibit interesting formations, and numerous beech trees exhibit graffiti (some authentic, some doubtful) from the turn of the century. Weverton Cliffs (0.11 mi. by side trail, at 5.85/0.88 mi.) offers a magnificent view of the Potomac River gorge.

Maps

PATC Map #6 and USGS Keedysville and Harpers Ferry Quadrangles

Campground

There is a camping area (by permit only) in Gathland State Park (at 0.14/6.59mi.). Register at Park office. Nightly fee is 50¢ per person for organized youth groups and *AT* thru-hikers; $1.00 for others.

Camping and fires are prohibited throughout this section, except at designated sites in the Park.

Supplies

Water is available only at Crampton Gap.

Brief Description

The historical interest in Crampton Gap and the view from Weverton Cliffs make this one of the most popular sections of the *AT* in Maryland. The Trail follows both the crest of the narrow ridge and the western rim, with little change in elevation, through a mature forest with excellent footing. North to south is easier because there is a net descent of 500 feet between Crampton Gap and Weverton.

Side Trails

To viewpoint (at 3.21/3.52 mi.)
To Weverton Cliffs (at 5.85/0.88 mi.)

Detailed Trail Data—North to South

0—Gapland Road (Md–572), in Gathland State Park, at Crampton Gap (originally "Crampton's Gap"). The park has *water,* rest rooms, phone, and a museum. *Camping and fires are prohibited throughout this section, except at designated sites in the Park.* (To left are historical markers and a memorial to Civil War newspaper correspondents, erected by George Alfred

Townsend, a Civil War journalist who used the pen name "Gath." Ahead is Gath Hall, of the Townsend estate, which was restored as a museum in 1958.) Ascend park driveway.

0.10—Turn left at parking lot and ascend gravel road. Pass Townsend's empty mausoleum on right and Park office on left.

0.14—Civil War earthworks may be seen a short distance straight ahead. Heavy fighting occurred here during the Battle of Crampton's Gap, Sept. 14, 1862. (The Federals, under Franklin, eventually overwhelmed the greatly outnumbered Confederates, under McLaws.) Turn right, then go right at fork just ahead. Left fork leads to designated camping area (by permit only). Thereafter, the Trail undulates along the ridge.

1.00—Pass dark red granite memorial to Glenn R. Caveney on left. (Caveney helped maintain this section of Trail with his father. He was killed in an auto accident and his father established a fund which was used to purchase a 4-acre tract surrounding the memorial, which was dedicated in March, 1976.)

1.46—Pass an impressive knoll, which exhibits an evenly fractured pile of rocks.

1.75—Brownsville Gap. Go straight across dirt road (see "Road Approaches"), then bear right just ahead as old road intersects on left.

1.78—Old road intersects on right. Go straight. Numerous beech trees here.

1.82—Cross buried coaxial cable.

2.81—Pass another impressive knoll, which exhibits oddly balanced rocks that are squarely stacked.

3.21—Blue-blazed trail leads 100 feet right to mediocre view of Pleasant Valley and Elk Ridge.

3.85—Turn left onto old road at junction.

4.01—Giant beech on right has oldest graffiti dates ("1892" and "1899") that have been found on beeches on this ridge.

4.62—Old road intersects on right. Go straight.

5.06—Go right at fork and descend, sometimes steeply, on a very rough path.

5.85—Turn right and descend steeply, by 16 well-engineered switchbacks, then more gradually. (Blue-blazed trail leads 0.11 mi. straight ahead to Weverton Cliffs. This magnificent view of the Potomac River gorge should not be missed. Set in stone at the Cliffs is a plaque in memory of Congressman Goodloe E. Byron, 1928–78, a great supporter of the *AT.*)

6.67—Cross paved Weverton Road and follow nameless road straight ahead.

6.73—Turn left at parking area on shoulder of road. To continue on the Trail, cross barrier and follow abandoned section of old highway.

Detailed Trail Data—South to North

0—Parking area. Follow nameless road toward ridge. *Camping and fires are prohibited throughout this section except for designated sites in Gathland State Park.*

0.06—Cross Weverton Road and enter woods. Ascend gradually, then steeply climb cliff by 16 well-engineered switchbacks.

0.88—Turn left and ascend, sometimes steeply, on a very rough path. (Blue-blazed trail leads 0.11 mi. right to Weverton Cliffs. This magnificent view of the Potomac River gorge should not be missed. Set in stone at the cliffs is a plaque to the memory of Congressman Goodloe E. Byron, 1928–78, a great supporter of the *AT.*)

1.67—Go straight, coming onto old road that intersects on right. Footing improves, and Trail undulates along rest of ridge.

2.11—Go right at fork.

2.72—Giant beech on left has oldest graffiti dates (''1892'' and ''1899'') that have been found on beeches on this ridge.

2.88—Turn right onto intersecting old road.

3.52—Blue-blazed trail leads 100 feet left to mediocre view of Pleasant Valley and Elk Ridge.

3.92—Pass an impressive knoll, which exhibits oddly balanced rocks that are squarely stacked.

4.91—Cross buried coaxial cable.

4.95—Go right at fork. Numerous beech trees here.

4.98—Brownsville Gap. Go left at fork, then cross dirt road (see ''Road Approaches'').

5.27—Pass another impressive knoll, which exhibits an evenly fractured pile of rocks.

5.73—Pass dark red granite memorial to Glenn R. Caveney on right. (Caveney helped maintain this section of Trail with his father. He was killed in an auto accident and his father established a fund that was used to purchase a 4-acre tract surrounding the memorial, which was dedicated in March, 1976.)

6.59—Pass designated camping area (by permit only; no other camping is allowed in Gathland State Park), descend gravel road, and turn left at junction. Path to right leads a short distance to Civil War earthworks. Heavy fighting occurred here during the Battle of Crampton's Gap, Sept. 14, 1862. (The Federals, under Franklin, eventually overwhelmed the greatly outnumbered Confederates, under McLaws.)

6.63—Turn right onto paved park driveway after passing Townsend's empty mausoleum and a parking lot. Park office is to right of parking lot.

6.73—Gapland Road (Md–572), in Gathland State Park, at Crampton Gap. The park has *water*, rest rooms, phone, and a museum. (To the right are historical markers and a memorial to Civil War newspaper correspondents, erected by George Alfred Townsend, a Civil War journalist who used the pen-name "Gath." On the hill to the south is Gath Hall, of the Townsend estate, which was restored as a museum in 1958.) To continue on the Trail, cross Md–572 and pass through gap in stone fence.

View from Weverton Cliffs

SECTION 7
WEVERTON TO HARPERS FERRY
Distance 3.29 Miles

Road Approaches and Parking

To reach Weverton: From US–340, take Md–67 north. Then take first right, turning onto nameless road. There is lots of room to park on right, in clearing beside abandoned section of old highway, at curve in road. The *AT,* going south, follows the abandoned section of old highway. Distance is 61 miles from Washington, D.C.

From US–Alt. 40, take Md–67 south. Then take the last left turn, onto nameless road, before reaching the US–340 junction. Then see above.

To reach Harpers Ferry: From US–340, turn onto Shenandoah St. (the "entrance" road for Harpers Ferry National Historical Park), at west end of bridge over Shenandoah River. Park in large lot on right; $5 fee per car. Then continue to end of Shenandoah St., turn right, and pass under trestle. The *AT,* going north, crosses the Potomac River on the Goodloe Byron Memorial Footbridge, on left. Distance is 61 miles from Washington, D.C.

Points of Interest

The Chesapeake & Ohio Canal is of historical interest, and the Goodloe Byron Memorial Footbridge offers a superb view of the Potomac River.

Maps

PATC Map #6 and USGS Harpers Ferry Quadrangle

Campgrounds

Weverton Primitive Camp (0.06 mi. by side trail, at 0.76/2.53 mi.), by the Potomac, has *no privy* (until 1987) and *no water* (the river is polluted), but is the only place where free camping is possible in this section. There is camping space in the yard of the Hostel. (See below.)

Public Accommodations

Harpers Ferry Hostel (formerly Kiwanis), operated by the Potomac Area Council of the American Youth Hostel, has been renovated and expanded to a 40-bed capacity (0.37 mi. by side trail, at 2.02/1.27 mi.; see Loudoun Heights Trail, in chapter on "Side Trails," for directions). It opens at 6:00 every night, all year. The hostel is equipped with bunks, toilets, showers, cooking facilities, and a phone, but does not provide meals. The per-night fees are $9 for members of AYH, ATC, or PATC; $12 for non-members; and $4 for camping in the large yard.

Supplies

There is a grocery store in Sandy Hook (0.04 mi. by side trail at 2.02/1.27 mi.). A motel and restaurant are near the Maryland end of the Sandy Hook Bridge.

Water and a telephone are available at the Hostel. (See above.)

Brief Description

For most of this section, the Trail utilizes the towpath along the abandoned Chesapeake & Ohio Canal, a National Historical Park. The level terrain and excellent footing make this the easiest section in this book. The scenery, with the Potomac River on one side and the canal on the other, offers a pleasant change from the adjoining ridges.

North to south: From Weverton, the *AT* descends slightly along Israel Creek and crosses the Baltimore & Ohio Railroad tracks. Then the Trail follows the Chesapeake & Ohio Canal towpath to the Goodloe Byron Memorial Footbridge, where it crosses the Potomac into Harpers Ferry.

South to north: From Harpers Ferry, the *AT* crosses the Potomac on the Goodloe Byron Memorial Footbridge and follows the Chesapeake & Ohio Canal towpath. Leaving the towpath, the Trail then crosses the Baltimore & Ohio Railroad tracks and ascends slightly along Israel Creek to Weverton.

Side Trails

To Weverton Primitive Camp (at 0.76/2.53 mi.)
Loudoun Heights Trail (at 2.02/1.27 mi.)

Detailed Trail Data—North to South

0—Parking area at Weverton. Cross guard rail and follow abandoned road. (This was part of Md-67 until a new interchange with US-340 was built in 1969.)

0.04—Bear right off abandoned road and enter woods ahead. Trail descends gradually with undulations. *Be careful of precipitous drop* to Israel Creek, on right.

0.17—Cross under US-340 overpass. A dirt "road" and pilings of a former bridge may be seen along Israel Creek. These mark the route of the former Washington County Railroad, which later became the Hagerstown Branch of the Baltimore & Ohio Railroad.

0.41—Cross paved road (old Md-180), go straight ahead, and cross Baltimore & Ohio Railroad tracks where they curve. Some toadflax flowers may be seen as one leaves the woods.

0.51—Cross causeway over abandoned Chesapeake & Ohio Canal, pass gate, and turn right onto towpath. (The 184.5 mile Canal, which linked Washington and Cumberland, was completed in 1850. Operation ended in 1924, after the Canal was severely damaged by a storm. The Canal is now a National Historical Park.) Trail blazes will be found on posts along the towpath. Ahead, pass a few private houses and several paths to the Potomac River.

0.76—Blue-blazed trail leads 0.06 mi. left to Weverton Primitive Camp. *No water;* the river is polluted.

2.02—Cross under Sandy Hook Bridge and continue on towpath. On right, blue-blazed Loudoun Heights Trail leads 3.19 mi. to rejoin the *AT* in Virginia Section 1. It passes a grocery store in Sandy Hook and the Harpers Ferry Hostel. (See chapter on "Side Trails.")

2.67—Pass canal lock on right.

3.11—Pass under the first of two trestles, turn left, and ascend metal stairs of Goodloe Byron Memorial Footbridge, which crosses the Potomac River. (Congressman Goodloe E. Byron, 1928–78, was a great supporter of the *AT.*) Hikers wishing to reach the Grant Conway and Elk Ridge trails should continue on the towpath. (See chapter on "Side Trails.")

3.29—Bulletin board, at end of brick walkway in Harpers

Ferry. An adjacent post bears map of *AT* route through town. Overlook on left has superb view of Potomac and Shenandoah confluence. To continue on the Trail, turn right and pass under trestle.

Detailed Trail Data—South to North

0—Bulletin board at beginning of brick walkway. Follow walkway to Goodloe Byron Memorial Footbridge and cross Potomac River. (Congressman Goodloe E. Byron, 1928–78, was a great supporter of the *AT.*) Overlook on right has superb view of Potomac and Shenandoah confluence.

0.18—Turn right onto Chesapeake & Ohio Canal towpath. (The 184.5 mile Canal, which linked Washington and Cumberland, was completed in 1850. Operation ended in 1924, after the canal was severely damaged by a storm. The Canal is now a National Historical Park.) Hikers wishing to reach the Grant Conway and Elk Ridge trails should turn left onto the towpath at this junction. (See chapter on "Side Trails.") Trail blazes will be found on posts along the towpath.

0.62—Pass canal lock on left.

1.27—On left, blue-blazed Loudoun Heights Trail leads 3.19 mi. to rejoin *AT* in Virginia Section 1. It passes a grocery store in Sandy Hook and the Harpers Ferry Hostel. (See chapter on "Side Trails.") Cross under Sandy Hook Bridge and continue on towpath.

2.53—Blue-blazed trail leads 0.06 mi. right to Weverton Primitive Camp. *No water;* the river is polluted.

2.78—Turn left off towpath and onto dirt road, pass gate, and cross causeway over canal.

2.81—Cross Baltimore & Ohio Railroad tracks. Then bear left and cross paved road (old Md–180), aiming at woods at tip of triangular piece of land bounded by loop of road.

2.88—Enter woods and ascend on undulating path. Some toadflax flowers may be seen here.

3.12—Cross under US–340 overpass. (A dirt "road" and pilings of a former bridge may be seen along Israel Creek, the deep ravine on the left. These mark the route of the former Washington County Railroad, which later became the Hagerstown

Branch of the Baltimore & Ohio Railroad.) Ahead, *be careful of precipitous drop* on left.

3.25—Turn left onto abandoned road. (This was part of Md–67 until a new interchange with US–340 was built in 1969.)

3.29—Cross guard rail, at parking area by Weverton. To continue on the Trail, turn right onto nameless paved road.

C&O Canal Towpath

CHAPTER 5
HARPERS FERRY
GENERAL INFORMATION

Harpers Ferry is one of the outstanding historical and scenic attractions on the *AT.* It became a National Historical Park in 1963. From north to south, the Trail passes through the scene of John Brown's raid, and then makes its way along the slope of a cliff, past the famous Jefferson Rock.

Two key *AT* offices are located in Harpers Ferry: (1) the headquarters of the Appalachian Trail Conference, and (2) the Appalachian Trail Project Office of the National Park Service.

HISTORY

Peter Stephens, a trader, settled in Harpers Ferry (then called "The Hole") in 1733 and established ferries across both rivers. Robert Harper purchased "squatter's rights" from Stephens and purchased the land, in 1747, from the legal holder, Lord Fairfax. The following spring, Fairfax engaged Peter Jefferson (father of Thomas) to survey the land. The survey party included fifteen-year-old George Washington, who later revisited this area several times before designating Harpers Ferry as the site for a national arsenal in 1796.

Beginning in the late 1700's water transportation was improved with by-pass canals around the rapids of the two rivers, and the C&O Canal along the Potomac to Georgetown (Washington, D.C.) began operations from Harpers Ferry in the early 1830's, providing access to tidewater markets. Early in the nineteenth century Harpers Ferry became an important transportation and industrial center, attracting a produce center, hotels, saloons and livery stables to service the town. The water-level gateway through the mountains also attracted the B&O R.R. which soon gave the C&O Canal strong competition, and eventually won out. Here, the Winchester and Potomac R.R. (now a branch of the B&O) joined the main line. Today, the towpath of the canal is "a natural" for a hiking trail. The towpath, across the Potomac from the town, leads downriver approximately 61 miles to Washington and upriver 124 miles to Cumberland.

An interesting historical and nature hike of 1.5 m. is found on Virginius Island (where some restoration work is being carried on by the Job Corps and the National Park Service). One of the National Park Service publications available at the Visitor Center provides a key to the numbered stakes along the trail and describes the natural and historical features. Here was the site of an industrial village: a cotton textile mill with gas lighting, sawmill, flour mill, iron foundry, rolling mill, carriage factory, oil mill, a rifle factory (introduced the system of interchangeable parts), and row dwelling houses. The entire industrial complex was dependent upon water power, the source for industrial energy in the early 1800's; the underground culverts which carried the intricate system of raceways may be traced. Devastated by flood, fire, and war, the area now approximates the natural conditions when the white man arrived. The rich verdure on the alluvial deposits now covers all but scattered vestiges of man's improvements.

Harpers Ferry never recovered from the John Brown raid in 1859 and the following Civil War. (The Brown raid and the role of Harpers Ferry in the Civil War are adequately covered in the free leaflet available at the Visitor Center.) In addition to war, fire, flood, and the pestilence (cholera and typhoid epidemics) ravaged the town. Technological advancements in power no longer made it necessary to locate factories at the water's edge where floods were a recurring threat.

Most of the town lay in ruins when the Harpers Ferry National Monument (a designation of the National Park Service) was provided for in a congressional enabling act of 1944. The first land was acquired in 1952, and the Harpers Ferry National Historical Park was created in 1963. In addition to the downtown facilities and Virginius Island, land extending to Loudoun Heights across the Shenandoah, Bolivar Heights, and Elk Ridge to a point beyond the Stone Fort in Maryland, have been added. The State of Virginia has not exercised its right by the 1944 Congressional enactment to provide land for the park.

POINTS OF INTEREST

Buildings in downtown Harpers Ferry are being restored, one by one, to the 1859–65 era. Currently, buildings and interior exhibits are open from 8 a.m. to 6 p.m. daily. The Visitor Center is located in the Stagecoach Inn (1826). A slide program and exhibits tell the history of Harpers Ferry and the story of John Brown's raid. (Rest rooms are located in the building adjacent to the Visitor Center.) The Master Armorer's House, down Shenandoah Street from the Visitor Center, contains an exhibit on gunmaking.

The fire engine house where Brown and his men made their last stand was located across Potomac Street on the site marked by a stone obelisk. (It was moved in March 1968 from the grounds of the Stephen Mather Training Center, where it was on the site now occupied by the modernistic Interpretation Center of the National Park Service. The Building has been moved many times since its removal from Harpers Ferry for a financially unsuccessful venture at the Columbian Exposition in Chicago in 1893. The present replica is slightly smaller than the original; many of the bricks were taken for souvenirs during the periods when it was dismantled.) The Park Service plans to move the building to its original location when negotiations with the B&O Railroad are completed.

Store windows along Shenandoah Street display merchandise of a century ago, as well as tools and artifacts unearthed in the restoration and archeological excavations. Foundations of the arsenal and a trench showing destroyed muskets are visible. (Press-button recording recites local history here.) The foundations of some of the rectangular armory buildings may be seen on the Potomac River side of the town in a neglected sunken garden adjacent to the relocated railroad station.

The *AT* passes the last house of Robert Harper. Built between 1775 and 1781, it is the oldest surviving structure in town. It was restored by the Park Service and furnished with period pieces by the Women's Clubs of the county. The building is open daily.

The *AT* also passes Jefferson Rock, which is on a bluff overlooking the Shenandoah and the gap across to Loudoun

Heights. The present Jefferson Rock is a flat stone supported by red sandstone pillars rising from a larger rock at the edge of the cliff.

The original rock associated with Jefferson was a balanced one. Captain Henry, a Federalist stationed at Harpers Ferry, and men of his company, stirred by Jefferson's campaign promise to reduce appropriations for defense in 1800, pried the large boulder loose and sent it crashing to the quarry below. Jefferson described the views in his "Notes on Virginia" in 1782:

"You stand on a very high point. . . . On your right comes up the Shenandoah. . . . On your left approaches the Potomac, in quest of a passage also. In the moment of their junction, they rush together against the mountain, render it asunder, and pass off to the sea. . . . For the mountain being cloven asunder, she presents to your eye, through the cleft, a small catch of smooth blue horizon, at an infinite distance of the plain country. . . . This scene is worth a voyage across the Atlantic. Yet here, as in the neighborhood of the Natural Bridge, are people who have passed their lives within a half a dozen miles, and have never been to survey these monuments of a war between rivers and mountains. . ."

Later, when Thomas Jefferson was President, he remembered an eagles' nest in a large oak seen from this vantage point and requested the Superintendent of the Arsenal to procure some eagles. Nailing slats on the trunk of the tree, the son of the Superintendent and two friends climbed the tree and captured three eaglets. Jefferson sent one of the young eagles to the King of Spain, who in turn gave the President an Andalusian ram. This early White House lawnmower delighted in chasing boys who teased him. The ram with the spreading horns was successful in one of his pursuits and the impact killed a young man by the name of Carr. The President sold the ram and thus Andalusian sheep were first introduced into this country.

The view of the merging of the two rivers from the present Jefferson Rock is partially obscured by buildings and trees. From a point where the two rivers merge, the spire of Chimney Rock may be discerned one-third of the way up Loudoun Heights.

For further information on the area, the Visitor Center on Shenandoah Street is recommended. Reference material in the form of books and magazine articles concerning Harpers Ferry are numerous.

REFERENCES

Joseph Barry, *The Strange Story of Harpers Ferry,* The Sheperdstown Register (W. Va.), 1958.

E. L. Bowen, *Rambles in the Path of the Steam Horse,* Philadelphia, Wm. Brownell and Wm. White Smith, 1854.

Philip S. Forner, *Basic Writings of Thomas Jefferson,* New York, Wiley, 1944.

Harpers Ferry

HARPERS FERRY SECTION
Distance 0.95 Miles

Road Approaches and Parking

From US-340, turn onto Shenandoah St. (the "entrance" road for Harpers Ferry National Historical Park), at west end of bridge over Shenandoah River. Park in large lot on right; $5 fee per car. Then continue on Shenandoah St. to intersection with Washington St. (no sign), the first street on left. The *AT,* going south from the opposite direction, turns here onto Washington St. (There is also room to park at the junction of US–340 and Shenandoah St. The *AT,* going north, ascends the cliff there.) Distance is 61 miles from Washington, D.C.

Maps

PATC Map #7 and USGS Harpers Ferry Quadrangle

Camping

Camping and fires *are prohibited* throughout this section.

Public Accommodations and Supplies

Harpers Ferry has a hotel, post office, and various stores and services. Detailed information can be obtained at the ATC Headquarters, open 9 a.m. to 5 p.m., seven days a week, in May through October; Monday through Friday during the rest of the year. (See "Detailed Trail Data" for directions.)

Side Trails

To ATC Headquarters (at 0.69/0.26 mi.)

Detailed Trail Data—North to South

0—Bulletin board, at end of brick walkway. An adjacent post bears map of *AT* route through town. Turn right and pass under trestle ahead. Overlook on left has superb view of Potomac and Shenandoah confluence. (The Trail is unmarked between here and the cliff, due to Park regulations. Along the cliff, metal plaques mark the Trail.)

0.04—Turn left onto Shenandoah St. (no sign), the first street past the trestle. (On left is replica of fire-engine house in which John Brown made his stand. Old Federal arsenal foundations are adjacent.) Go one block on Shenandoah St., passing building with "John Brown Story" sign.

0.08—Turn right onto Washington St. (no sign). (The Park Visitor Center is straight ahead on Shenandoah St.)

0.10—Turn left past first house on left and ascend stairway very steeply. (To reach the ATC Headquarters and a post office, continue on Washington St. about 0.5 mi. to its intersection with Jackson St. ATC is on the left corner. A post office is two blocks farther, at the junction of Washington, Union, and Franklin streets.)

0.12—Pass "Armory Workers' Apartments" on right.

0.14—Go straight ahead up road. Robert Harper's house, the oldest in Harpers Ferry (1775–81), is on right corner here. Ahead, on left, pass St. Peter's Roman Catholic Church (1833).

0.17—Go straight up stairs, leaving road, where road bears to right.

0.19—Pass ruins of St. John's Episcopal Church (1852) on right.

0.24—Go right at fork onto path marked by "Harper Cemetery" sign. (Left path leads a few yards to excellent view from Jefferson Rock.)

0.28—Go straight at cross-paths. (Path on right leads a few yards to Harper Cemetery.) Ahead, the Trail undulates along the cliff. *Watch for poison ivy.*

0.43—Go straight. (Path on right leads to Storer College campus.) Stay on cliff and ignore intersecting paths ahead.

0.69—Blue-blazed trail leads 0.28 mi. right to ATC headquarters. Go straight.

0.70—Go right at fork.

0.95—Junction of US-340 and Shenandoah St. To continue on the Trail, cross bridge over Shenandoah River via narrow pedestrian-walk.

NOTE: The Trail will soon be relocated, so as to loop under the bridge, in order to eliminate the highway crossing.

Detailed Trail Data—South to North

0—Junction of US-340 and Shenandoah St. Cross guard-rail and ascend cliff very steeply at first. Marked by sign that reads: "Cliff Trail, ATC." *Watch for poison ivy.* (Only metal plaques mark the Trail along the cliff. The Trail is unmarked through the town, due to Park regulations.)

0.25—Path intersects on right. Go straight.

0.26—Blue-blazed trail leads 0.28 mi. left to ATC Headquarters. (To reach ATC and post office, turn left at level clearing and follow path to back of massive brick building. Then follow service road past tennis/basketball court, turn left onto Fillmore St. at crossroads, and turn right onto Jackson St. after one block. ATC Headquarters is on corner of Jackson and Washington Streets. Post office is two blocks to left on Washington St., at junction with Union and Franklin Streets.) Go straight. Trail undulates ahead. Stay on cliff and ignore intersecting paths.

0.52—Go right at fork. (Path on left leads to Storer College campus.)

0.67—Go straight at cross-paths. (Path on left leads a few yards to Harper Cemetery.) Descend, sometimes very steeply.

0.71—Go straight. (Path on right leads a few yards to excellent view from Jefferson Rock.)

0.77—Pass ruins of St. John's Episcopal Church (1852) on left and descend stairs.

0.78—Go straight onto paved road. Ahead, pass St. Peter's Roman Catholic Church (1833) on right.

0.81—Where road bears to left, go straight down stairs. Robert Harper's house, the oldest in Harpers Ferry (1775–81), is on left corner here.

0.83—Pass "Armory Workers' Apartments" on left.

0.85—Bottom of stairs. Turn right onto Washington St.

0.87—Turn left onto Shenandoah St. and go one block. (The Park Visitor Center is to right on Shenandoah St.)

0.91—Turn right and pass under trestle ahead. (On right is replica of fire-engine house in which John Brown made his stand. Old Federal arsenal foundations are adjacent.)

0.95—Turn left at bulletin board at beginning of brick walkway. (Straight ahead, overlook has superb view of Potomac and Shenandoah confluence.) To continue on the Trail, follow brick walkway to Goodloe Byron Memorial Footbridge.

Maryland AT

CHAPTER 6
NORTHERN VIRGINIA AND WEST VIRGINIA
GENERAL INFORMATION
Distance 57.26 Miles

This segment of the *AT* begins at the western end of the bridge over the Shenandoah River at Harpers Ferry. For about 14 miles, it follows the ridge crest that forms the boundary between Virginia and West Virginia. It zigzags across the state-line, with its total mileage in West Virginia (exclusive of Harpers Ferry) somewhat over 6 miles.

After a steep climb from the river bank to the crest, the Trail follows the narrow crest of the Blue Ridge south past ruined stone breastworks of the Civil War period, through a section frequently burned over. This was the first section of Trail that was constructed, in 1927–28, by the PATC. Some of this area is now included in the Harpers Ferry National Historical Park.

On each side of Snickers Gap, the *AT* skirts a long-established summer community. From Crescent Rock to Ashby Gap, land closings have forced the Trail off the main ridge and onto a route that crosses a succession of side ridges and hollows. Within this section, the *AT* passes Mount Weather, a classified government installation.

For similar reasons, the Trail snakes along the slopes on each side of the Blue Ridge from Ashby Gap to Manassas Gap. The relocation of the Trail in these two sections represents one of the PATC's foremost successes in Trail protection.

South of Manassas Gap, the Trail climbs, east of Linden, over an abandoned, mountain-top farm, with fine views, and passes over the slopes of High Knob before descending to the west of Chester Gap. Then the Trail passes through the woods and fields of Harmony Hollow, on the western side of the Blue Ridge, to Shenandoah National Park.

From north to south, the Blue Ridge changes from a narrow ridge to a wider expanse of side ridges and outlying mountains. This is accompanied by an increase in the variety of growth that can be seen along the Trail.

The Trail in this chapter has been divided into the following sections:

1. Harpers Ferry to Keys Gap .... 5.33 mi.
2. Keys Gap to Snickers Gap .... 13.45 mi.
3. Snickers Gap to Ashby Gap .... 13.75 mi.
4. Ashby Gap to Manassas Gap .... 12.50 mi.
5. Manassas Gap to US–522 .... 8.39 mi.
6. US–522 to Shenandoah National Park .... 3.84 mi.

HISTORY ALONG THE TRAIL

The first part of the Appalachian Trail to be established between the Hudson Valley and the Great Smokies was opened south of Harpers Ferry in 1927 by the newly formed Potomac Appalachian Trail Club. Within two years, a handful of members had made the Trail a reality as far as Rockfish Gap. Their work inspired the formation of other groups, which completed other links in the 2,000-mile footpath.

The PATC appointed its first trail overseer in this region. Within two years of its opening, the original section of Trail was nearly lost because of fire, undergrowth and neglect. Walter R. Jex was assigned to maintain the *AT* from Harpers Ferry to Bluemont, a distance of 18 miles. Other PATC members soon took responsibility for other Trail sections, and the system of Trail overseers was born.

Early History

History in the conventional sense has happened only in bits and pieces along the Trail south of Harpers Ferry, while to the west in the Shenandoah Valley it has occurred on the grand scale. The natural barrier of the Blue Ridge has helped to channel settlement, commerce, and even war into the great flow of history up and down the valley. Along the Trail, however, we speak more of men crossing the ridge on missions of importance to the lands below.

Before the coming of the white man, this region was sparsely settled by tribes of the Powhatan Confederation to the east and by the Shawnees to the west. Other tribes, mentioned in the

Maryland section of this Guide, used two great trails for war and migration. East of the ridge in Loudoun and Fauquier Counties was the Great War Road. To the west in the Shenandoah Valley was the major Indian trail that later became the chief route for white men as well; that trail is now known locally as the Valley Pike and more generally as U.S. Route 11.

The first explorer to cross the Blue Ridge was a German, John Lederer, who made three successive trips to the Blue Ridge in March and May of 1669 and in August of 1670. On this last trip he discovered the northern pass into the Valley, probably Chester Gap, since he ascended the Rappahannock. The monument commemorating his discovery is located at Manassas Gap, however, just off the *AT* at Linden, Va. In 1707, the French explorer Louis Michelle led a party from Maryland into the Shenandoah Valley at Harpers Ferry and traveled as far south as the Massanuttens.

Settlement in the Blue Ridge began in the 1720's when German immigrants moved south from Pennsylvania, taking up land in the middle section of the Valley. The lower Valley was not fully settled until after the French and Indian War, when Virginia planters moved in from the Tidewater.

The Appalachian Trail in northern Virginia and West Virginia lies within the original grant of Charles II to the Lords Fairfax, which conveyed all lands between the Potomac and Rappahannock Rivers. Much was sold for settlement (and some taken by squatters), but in 1736 Thomas Lord Fairfax ordered a 120,000-acre tract surveyed, which he established as his Manor of Leeds. This included the entire Blue Ridge from Snickers Gap to Chester Gap and much of the Shenandoah Valley adjacent to it. When Fairfax settled in Virginia in 1748, he built his manor house, Greenway Court, near White Post. His surveyor that year was a 16-year-old lad named George Washington.

The Manor of Leeds was subsequently divided into lesser manors, all of which figured in speculation during the region's first land boom. A syndicate consisting of John Marshall, James Marshall, and their brother-in-law Raleigh Colston, acquired the Manor in 1793. A clouded title prevented them from selling land, however, nearly bringing financial ruin until the courts cleared the title in 1806.

Blue Ridge Gaps

Five gaps in the Blue Ridge have always provided the essential contacts in northern Virginia between the Piedmont and the Shenandoah Valley. Known by various names in the past, they are now called Keys Gap, Snickers Gap, Ashby Gap, Manassas Gap, and Chester Gap.

Keys Gap, formerly Vestals Gap, was served by a ferry on the Shenandoah as early as 1747, where at that time the region had its first iron industry. Washington used this route in 1754 during the campaign to Great Meadows and Fort Necessity, as did part of Braddock's army in 1755. (The name has variously been spelled Keys and Keyes; in February 1964, however, the Board of Geographic Names of the U.S. Geological Survey decided on Keys.)

Snickers Gap was named for Edward Snicker, who operated a ferry across the Shenandoah before 1764. It was originally known as Williams Gap, but has had its present name through most of its history. Snicker's name did not stick to the ferry, however, which became known as Castleman's. Washington used this route in his later years when he visited his cousin at Berryville and his brothers at Charles Town.

Ashby Gap was originally called the Upper Thoroughfare of the Blue Ridge and was served at the Shenandoah by Berry's Ferry. The main road to the valley, the Winchester Pike, passed through the gap, and it was along this route that Washington traveled on his first trip to the valley in 1748. Cornwallis' captured troops were marched through the gap to Winchester in 1781.

Ashby Gap received its present name from the Indian fighter, Col. John Ashby, whose family settled near what is now Paris. The name also brings to mind his noted descendent General Turner Ashby, Confederate cavalry leader under General Stonewall Jackson.

Manassas Gap (or Manassa's Gap) was at one time known as Calmes Gap, after Marquis Calmes, a colonial figure whose name also appears on a bend of the Shenandoah River known as Calmes Neck.

Chester Gap once went by the name Happy Creek Gap.

Backpackers on the AT

Railroad Development

These gaps naturally attracted considerable interest during the railroad building era, especially after the B&O preempted the Potomac water-level route at Harpers Ferry. Because of its low elevation, Manassas Gap was the most attractive, and by 1854 a railroad by that name ran from its junction with the Orange and Alexandria Railroad at Manassas through the gap to Strasburg in the Valley.

One other railroad scheme involved both Keys Gap and Snickers Gap. This is remembered by many area residents as the Washington & Old Dominion Railroad, which served Bluemont from 1900 to 1939. The railroad originated in the 1840's as the Alexandria, Loudoun & Hampshire Railroad, which was to reach Winchester by way of Vestal's (Keys) Gap. Financial troubles dogged the line, and it had only reached the Catoctin Ridge by the Civil War. After a change in name to Washington, Ohio & Western ("WOW"), a change in route to Snickers Gap, and receivership, the rails finally came to Snickersville in 1900. That same year the town adopted the more euphonious name of Bluemont.

Construction of the railroad to Bluemont may have influenced the building of many turn-of-the-century summer homes in the Bluemont area. This early development made it difficult to locate a route for the Appalachian Trail when it was later established.

Civil War Action

The Blue Ridge figured prominently in many Civil War actions. Jackson marched his troops through Ashby Gap on July 18, 1861, prior to the First Battle of Bull Run. They bivouacked at Paris before boarding the Manassas Gap Railroad to reach the battle just in time.

A year later, in September 1862, Confederate troops under Jackson's command climbed Loudoun Heights to bombard Harpers Ferry and forced its surrender with 11,000 Union troops just before the Battle of Antietam. Also on Loudoun Heights, the Confederate raider, Col. John S. Mosby, attempted to overrun a sleeping encampment of Maryland Cavalry on January 10, 1864. He was discovered before he could spring the attack and was repulsed by half-dressed Union soldiers after a sharp fight which resulted in four deaths on each side.

To the south, Snickers Gap witnessed the retreat of General Jubal Early in July 1864, after his raid on Washington, D.C. In this gap in November 1864 Union troops laid an ambush for John Mobley, a former Mosby follower who led his own band to harass Union forces around Harpers Ferry. His death was largely due to information received after a $1,000 reward was put on his head.

The entire region from Snickers Gap to Manassas Gap and east to the Bull Run Mountains was under the influence of Col. Mosby, the "gray ghost," and soon earned the name "Mosby's Confederacy." Mosby's men lived in farmhouses throughout the region and gathered on command for their operations. Paris and Linden were frequent rendezvous sites.

South of Ashby Gap is Signal Knob, one of several promontories in the region used regularly for communications by both sides during the Civil War.

Scientific Activities

After the war, the most notable developments on the Blue Ridge occured near Snickers Gap and brought science to the forefront. In October 1868, near Bears Den Rocks, Dr. Mahlon Loomis conducted one of the most significant but unrecognized experiments of the time, whereby he nearly discovered the existence of radio waves and operated the first radio antenna. He and a colleague on Catoctin Ridge, 18 miles away, simultaneously raised kites with copper gauze attached, on a copper wire, which was attached to a galvanometer. In a prearranged sequence, the two men attached one or the other galvanometer to ground wires and secured readings on the opposite instrument. Loomis thought of electricity as being like an ocean with a force that resembled waves or ripples; his purpose was to develop a form of aerial telegraph. This experiment took place 20 years before Hertz demonstrated the existence of radio waves.

In 1900 Professor Willis L. Moore, Chief of the U.S. Weather Bureau, proposed bringing together on the Blue Ridge a number of advanced weather research activities; thus in 1901 Mount Weather began operation with the eventual goal of investigating terrestrial magnetism, thermodynamics of the atmosphere, solar-physical and upper air phenomena, and model weather research. Work did not get underway uniformly on all projects, but early in 1907 the Mount Weather Station achieved the highest (five miles) ascent of a kite ever achieved. This ascent provided invaluable instrument recordings on the upper atmosphere. After 1907, however, the Mount Weather project languished, and occasional proposals were offered to revive the facility for various purposes. One such was to make it a summer White House during the Coolidge Administration. In recent years, Mount Weather has been developed as a classified government installation, and is closed to public entry.

West of the Appalachian Trail in Chester Gap is another Government installation with an interesting past. It was originally acquired by the U.S. Army in 1911 as a remount station to provide a supply of horses and mules. Later it served as a prisoner-of-war camp, and was also used for training K-9 dogs. Its usefulness to the Army diminished after the war, and in 1948 the property was transferred to the U.S. Department of Agriculture which used it as a beef cattle research station and conference center. These operations were discontinued in the early 1970's, and the facility and land were transferred to the National Zoological Park (for a Research and Conservation Center) and to Virginia Polytechnic Institute (for a 4-H center).

Trail Route Status

Although the *AT* route in northern Virginia and West Virginia was one of the earliest parts of the Trail, this does not mean that the route is well established. From the start, relatively little was on public property. Some private property owners have, over the years, been increasingly reluctant to have the Trail cross their property. Where a key piece of property is involved, long sections of Trail have been effectively blocked.

In the last few years the National Park Service land acquisition program has protected a permanent, woodland route for nearly the entire northern Virginia and West Virginia stretch. This protection effort was aided by key purchases by the PATC in the early stages, and by the cooperation of the state of Virginia.

WEST VIRGINIA HISTORY

In 1863 West Virginia became a state, and Jefferson County, Virginia became a part of the new state. Along the state line the Appalachian Trail meanders back and forth using the best geographical features of the top of the Blue Ridge.

SELECTED REFERENCES

Davis, Julia, *The Shenandoah,* Rinehart & Co., N.Y., 1945.

Harwood, Herbert H. Jr., *Rails to the Blue Ridge,* Pioneer American Society, Falls Church, Va., 1969.

Leighton, Marion, "Mosby's Confederacy," *PATC Bulletin,* January 1939.

Loudoun County Civil War Centennial Commission, *Loudoun County and the Civil War: A History and Guide,* Leesburg, Va., 1961.

Schairer, Frank, *"Early Days of the Appalachian Trail,"* *PATC Bulletin,* July–September 1969.

Solyom, Herbert L., "Mount Weather," *PATC Bulletin,* January 1941.

Strain, Paula, "Kite String Antenna," *PATC Bulletin,* October–December 1968.

Wayland, John W., *Twenty-five Chapters on the Shenandoah Valley,* Shenandoah Publishing House, Strasburg, Va. 1957.

Wellman, Manley Wade, *Harpers Ferry, Prize of War,* McNally, Charlotte, N.C., 1960.

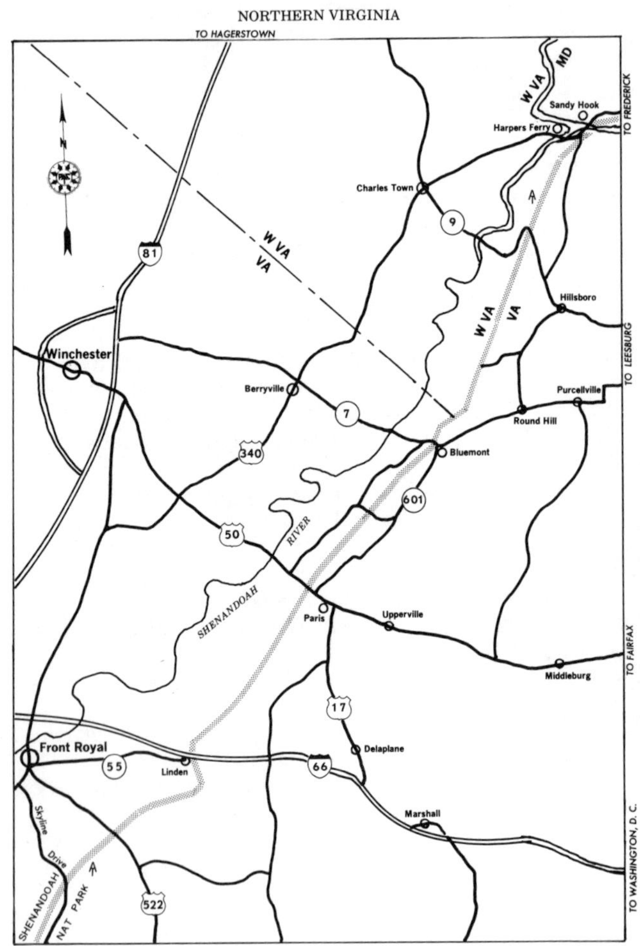
NORTHERN VIRGINIA
TO HAGERSTOWN
W VA
MD
Sandy Hook
Harpers Ferry
TO FREDERICK
N
Charles Town
9
W VA
VA
81
Hillsboro
W VA
VA
Winchester
TO LEESBURG
Berryville
Purcellville
7
Round Hill
Bluemont
340
601
50
RIVER
SHENANDOAH
Paris
Upperville
TO FAIRFAX
Middleburg
17
Front Royal
Delaplane
55
Linden
66
Marshall
Skyline
Drive
SHENANDOAH
NAT PARK
522
TO WASHINGTON, D. C.

SECTION 1
HARPERS FERRY TO KEYS GAP
Distance 5.33 Miles

Road Approaches and Parking

Harpers Ferry: This section of the *AT,* going south, starts at the junction of US–340 and Shenandoah St. (the "entrance" road for Harpers Ferry National Historical Park), at west end of bridge over Shenandoah River. There is room for a few cars to park at this junction. Distance is 61 miles from Washington, D.C.

Keys Gap: This is on Route 9. The *AT* crosses the highway in West Virginia, about 40 yards from the state-line. There is room for several cars to park beside the Trail, on the northern side of the highway. Hillsboro, Va., is 6 miles east; Charles Town, W. Va., is 7.4 miles west. It is about 52 miles from Washington, D.C.

Points of Interest

There are two excellent viewpoints at 1.13/4.20 mi. (via a 0.4 mi. side trail) and 3.74/1.59 mi. Several rock redoubts, built as Civil War defenses for Harpers Ferry, may be seen beside the Trail between 1.44/3.89 mi. and 1.66/3.67 mi.

Camping

Camping and fires *are prohibited* in the Park.

Maps

PATC Map #7 and USGS Harpers Ferry and Charles Town Quadrangles

Supplies

There is a grocery store and a telephone beside a gas station on Route 9, a short distance west from Keys Gap. A second store is located 0.1 mi. east. *Water* is available at the western store.

Brief Description

This is a relatively easy section, especially for northbound hikers, who face a net descent of about 600 feet. The footing is good, except for a rough 1.3 mi. segment.

North to south: From Harpers Ferry, the *AT* follows US-340 over the Shenandoah River and then ascends to the crest of Loudoun Heights, where it leaves Harpers Ferry National Historical Park. Thereafter, the Trail follows the ridge crest on paths and old roads, with two small dips at saddles and only one view.

South to north: From Keys Gap, the *AT* follows the ridge crest on old roads and paths, with two small dips at saddles and only one view. After entering Harpers Ferry National Historical Park, the Trail descends the west slope of Loudoun Heights to US-340, which it follows across the Shenandoah River.

Side Trails

To viewpoint (at 1.13/4.20 mi.)
Loudoun Heights Trail (at 1.44/3.89 mi.)

Detailed Trail Data—North to South

0—Junction of US-340 and Shenandoah St. While facing traffic, cross bridge over Shenandoah River via narrow pedestrian-walk. The Trail ahead lies within the Harpers Ferry National Historical Park.

Camping and fires are prohibited in the Park.

NOTE: The Trail will soon be relocated, so as to loop under the bridge, in order to eliminate the highway crossing.

0.28—End of bridge. Cross to right side of US-340 and ascend stairs on cliff. Splendid view ahead.

NOTE: The Trail to the ridge crest may be relocated in places.

0.45—Cross ravine filled with hemlocks.

0.66—Cross ravine and ascend through beautiful, profuse growth of periwinkle. *Follow blazes carefully.*

0.78—Cross WVa-32.

0.88—Turn left. Trail parallels old gullied road.

0.93—Trail joins gullied road.

1.13—Turn right onto *path* at junction of two old roads.

(Straight ahead on road, orange blazes lead about 0.4 mi. to rock outcrop with fine view.)

1.27—Turn right onto old road.

1.33—Turn left, off road and onto path, where bulldozed mounds of earth block road.

1.44—Ridge crest. Turn right at junction. On left, blue-blazed Loudoun Heights Trail leads 3.19 mi. to rejoin the *AT* in Maryland Section 7. (See chapter on "Side Trails.") Ahead, leave Harpers Ferry National Historical Park and pass rock redoubts dating from the Civil War. (When Lee invaded Maryland in 1862, he detailed Jackson to capture Harpers Ferry, which fell after a short siege, Sept. 13–15. Brigadier General John G. Walker's division bombarded the town from these heights. The redoubts were infantry defenses built and abandoned by the Federals.)

1.66—Pass concrete and metal foundation of some former structure, in clearing on right.

2.21—Ascend steeply.

2.50—Level, with rocky footing ahead.

3.31—Possible campsite on left. Descend.

3.74—Cross high-tension powerline. Excellent views to west and east. Shenandoah River can be seen from Trail here. Footing becomes good again.

3.93—Go left at fork and descend. (Former *AT* route leads right 0.08 mi. to intermittent Bear Pond.)

4.16—Ascend.

4.87—Level, then descend ahead.

4.93—Cross old road and almost immediately turn left onto another old road.

5.13—Go left at fork. Pass pasture on left just ahead as Trail parallels barbed-wire fence.

5.33—WVa–9 in Keys Gap. (There is a grocery store and telephone beside a gas station on WVa–9, a short distance to right. *Water* is available there. Another store is to left on WVa–9.) To continue on the Trail, cross WVa–9.

NOTE: Keys Gap Shelter may be moved to the north side of the gap.

Detailed Trail Data—South to North

0—WVa–9 in Keys Gap. From the highway, follow Trail along west edge of lawn and then enter woods. Ahead, pass pasture on right as Trail parallels barbed-wire fence. (There is a grocery store and telephone beside a gas station on WVa–9, a short distance to left. *Water* is available there. Another store is to right on WVa–9.)

NOTE: Keys Gap Shelter may be moved to the north side of the gap.

0.20—Old road intersects on left. Go straight and ascend ahead.

0.40—Go left at fork, then turn right off road and cross other branch of fork.

0.46—Level, then descend ahead.

1.17—Ascend.

1.40—Bear right as former *AT* route intersects on left. (Old *AT* route leads 0.08 mi. to intermittent Bear Pond.)

1.53—Cross high-tension powerline. Excellent views to west and east. Shenandoah River can be seen from Trail just ahead. Footing becomes rocky.

2.02—Possible campsite on right. Level.

2.83—Footing becomes good again. Descend steeply.

3.12—Ascend.

3.67—Pass concrete and metal foundation of some former structure, in clearing on left. Ahead, pass several rock redoubts dating from the Civil War. (When Lee invaded Maryland in 1862, he detailed Jackson to capture Harpers Ferry, which fell after a short siege, Sept. 13–15. Brigadier General John G. Walker's division bombarded the town from these heights. The redoubts were infantry defenses built and abandoned by the Federals.)

3.89—The *AT* enters Harpers Ferry National Historical Park. *Camping and fires are prohibited.* Turn left and descend. (Straight ahead, blue-blazed Loudoun Heights Trail leads 3.19 mi. to rejoin the *AT* in Maryland Section 7. See chapter on "Side Trails.")

NOTE: The Trail to US–340 may be relocated in places.

4.00—Turn right onto old road, near bulldozed mounds of earth.

4.06—Turn left off road and onto path.

4.20—Turn sharply left onto old gullied road and descend very steeply. (Orange blazes lead right about 0.4 mi. up this road to rock outcrop with fine view.)

4.40—Trail diverges to right of road, which it continues to parallel. Descend less steeply.

4.45—Turn right, away from road.

4.55—Cross WVa-32 and descend on path through beautiful, profuse growth of periwinkle. *Follow blazes carefully.*

4.67—Cross ravine.

4.88—Cross ravine filled with hemlocks. Splendid view from cliff ahead.

5.05—Turn left onto US-340. While facing traffic, cross bridge over Shenandoah River via narrow pedestrian-walk. Then cross to right side of US-340.

NOTE: The Trail will soon be relocated, so as to loop under the bridge, in order to eliminate the highway crossing.

5.33—Junction of US-340 and Shenandoah St. (the Park "entrance" road) in Harpers Ferry. To continue on the Trail, ascend cliff very steeply.

SECTION 2
KEYS GAP TO SNICKERS GAP
Distance 13.45 Miles

Road Approaches and Parking

Keys Gap: This is on Route 9. The *AT* crosses the highway in West Virginia, about 40 yards from the state-line. There is room for several cars to park beside the Trail, on the northern side of the highway. Hillsboro, Va., is 6 miles east; Charles Town, W. Va., is 7.4 miles west. It is about 52 miles from Washington, D.C.

To reach Blackburn Trail Center: From Va–7 or Va–9, take Va–719. Turn onto Va–713 and follow it almost to the top of the ridge, avoiding all private driveways.

Snickers Gap: This is on Va–7. The *AT* crosses Va–7 slightly west of the gap. There is room for numerous cars to park at the old rock crushers, on the southwest corner of Va–7 and Va–601. Several cars can park where *AT* leaves Va–679. There is also room for four cars to park on the *right shoulder only* of Va–601, 1.72 miles north of Va–7, by a junction with a dirt road on the left. From here, the *AT* can be reached by following the intersecting dirt road a half-mile to its junction with the *AT* at 10.62/2.83 mi. From Snickers Gap, Bluemont is 0.8 of a mile east, and Washington, D.C., is about 52 miles east.

Points of Interest

There are good-to-excellent views from a cleared hill by a CATV tower (at 2.01/11.44 mi.), from Buzzard Rocks (at 3.56/9.89 mi.) from an outcrop (at 6.09/7.36 mi.), from Crescent Rock (at 10.87/2.58 mi.), which also has unusual rock formations, and from outcrops (at 11.78/1.67 and 12.87/0.58 mi.). Other points of geological interest are The Lookout (at 6.83/6.62 mi.) and Devils Racecourse (at 10.28/3.12 mi.). The misnamed Laurel Swamp (at 5.25/8.20 mi.) has a beautiful growth of periwinkle and a former house site.

Maps

PATC Map #7 and USGS Charles Town, Round Hill, and Bluemont Quadrangles

Shelters and Campground

Keys Gap Shelter (0.04 mi. by side trail, at 0.12/13.33 mi.), built by the PATC in 1942–43, accommodates six persons. Spring is polluted. *Water* available at Keys Gap store.

Blackburn Center Campground (0.11 mi. by side trail, at 6.18/7.27 mi.), owned and maintained by the PATC, has a privy, fire ring, grill, and picnic table. Use is free on a first-come, first-served basis. *Water* is available at the Blackburn Center.

Blackburn Trail Center (0.27 mi. by side trail, at 6.41/7.04 mi.) is a house and two outbuildings owned and maintained by the PATC as a work center and recreation site. Club members are often present. Posted Trail information, logbook, a pay-phone, and *water* are available within the screened, but unlocked, porch. The Center's Hodgson House, a primitive cabin (beds and woodstove only), sleeps eight; open all year for free to *AT* thru-hikers.

Supplies

There are grocery stores on both sides of the Trail at Keys Gap including one with a telephone beside a gas station. Water may be obtained at these stores.

Water and a telephone are available at Blackburn Center (0.27 mi. by side trail, at 6.41/7.04 mi.).

Water is also available from *Sand Spring* (0.11 mi. on a loop trail, at 10.28/3.12 mi.), and sometimes from the intermittent *Laurel Spring* (at 5.30/8.15 mi.).

There is a post office in Bluemont, which has a General Delivery mail-drop that can be used by hikers.

Brief Description

This section offers an interesting hike with considerable variety. The length, numerous undulations, and occasional rocky footing make it one of the most rugged sections in this book. It is a moderately difficult day-hike.

North to south: From Keys Gap, the *AT* follows old roads, with short connecting links, sometimes along the ridge crest and sometimes on either side. The Trail crosses three knolls and passes a former house site before coming to the side trail to the

Blackburn Center, which is almost exactly in the middle of the section. After following the ridge crest for a mile, the Trail descends to Wilson Gap. Then the Trail climbs steeply over two more knolls and steeply descends a side ridge to Devils Racecourse. After ascending steeply through a saddle below Raven Rocks, the Trail passes Crescent Rock and very steeply descends 500 feet into Raven Rocks Hollow. Climbing only halfway out, the Trail skirts the slope of an outlying ridge and crosses the smaller Pigeon Hollow before reaching Va–679, which it follows to Va–7 slightly west of Snickers Gap.

South to north: From Va–7, slightly west of Snickers Gap, the *AT* follows Va–679 briefly before ascending into the woods. After crossing Pigeon Hollow, the Trail skirts the slope of an outlying ridge and descends very steeply into Raven Rocks Hollow. A very steep, 500-foot ascent takes the Trail past Crescent Rock to a saddle below Raven Rocks. Next the Trail descends steeply to Devils Racecourse. After returning to the main ridge by a steep ascent, the Trail crosses two knolls and descends steeply to Wilson Gap. Then the Trail ascends steeply to the ridge crest, which it follows for a mile. Along the crest, the Trail passes the side trail to the Blackburn Center, which is almost exactly in the middle of the section. In the section's northern half, the Trail follows old roads, with short connecting links, sometimes along the ridge crest and sometimes on either side. The Trail passes a former house site and crosses three more knolls before reaching Keys Gap.

Side Trails

To Keys Gap Shelter (at 0.12/13.33 mi.)

To Buzzard Rocks (at 3.56/9.89 mi.)

To Blackburn Center & Campground (at 6.18/7.27 mi. and 6.41/7.04 mi.)

To Sand Spring (at 10.28/3.12 mi.)

To Crescent Rock (at 10.91/2.54 mi.)

To spring (at 11.24/2.17 mi.)

Detailed Trail Data—North to South

0—WVa–9 in Keys Gap. Follow path with wire fence and field

on left. (There is a grocery store and telephone beside a gas station on WVa–9, a short distance to right. *Water* is available there. Another store is to left on WVa–9.)

0.12—Stock pond in field on left. Former spring on left is polluted. Blue-blazed trail leads right 0.04 mi. to Keys Gap Shelter. Ascend on old road ahead.

0.67—Old road intersects on right. Go straight.

1.12—Go left at fork.

1.58—Go left at fork.

1.66—Cross old road and bear right as another old road intersects on left.

1.72—Go right at fork and ascend steeply. *This is easy to miss.*

2.01—Turn right onto old road at junction, then go left at fork just ahead. (Up hill to right, road leads 70 yards to excellent view from cleared crest near CATV tower.)

2.14—Winter view to east. Ahead, descend through a very young forest on western side of crest.

3.00—Bear right off road and make short, very steep, ascent. Then descend.

3.18—Slight eastward view. Just ahead, pass what appears to be a small remnant of a chimney, a few yards to right.

3.31—Ascend steeply.

3.56—Unblazed path leads right 0.08 mi. to Buzzard Rocks. (Path forks. Right branch leads to scree with no view. Left branch leads to Buzzard Rocks, with excellent view of Shenandoah River and Shannondale Lake. Good site for one tent near view.) *AT* descends very steeply over boulder ahead, then more moderately.

3.68—Ascend generally with rocky footing.

4.06—Level. The Deer Lick, a mossy area not visible from the Trail, is on left a short distance before this point.

4.23—Descend.

4.54—Bear left onto old Shannondale Road (which intersects as a path on the right), then turn right off road just ahead. (The road once connected Hillsboro to Shannondale Springs, a famous 19th-century resort that was patronized by Presidents.)

4.85—Ascend along eastern side of ridge crest.

5.15—Descend.

5.25—The misnamed "Laurel Swamp." Beautiful, profuse growth of periwinkle covers former house site on right. Rock walls outline yard, and slight chimney ruins are visible. Garden terraces rise above the site.

5.30—Path leads right a few yards to walled-in *Laurel Spring,* which is often dry. Ascend.

6.09—Quartzite cliff on right offers good view.

6.18—Blue-blazed trail on left descends very steeply to campground (left fork in 0.11 mi.) and to Blackburn Trail Center, in 0.28 mi. *Water* is available (not dependable in winter) from Blackburn Center. An easier route to the Center is 0.23 mi. ahead. Descend generally ahead.

6.41—Blue-blazed trail on left leads to Blackburn Trail Center in 0.27 mi.

6.83—Pass The Lookout, an unusual pile of boulders on left. This once offered a fine eastward view, hence the name, but trees have now completely blocked the view.

6.86—Come into old road. (Short distance to right, road ends at clearing with good view.)

7.17—Path leads right to winter view from rocks. Descend steeply.

7.43—Go right, off road and onto path, at fork in Wilson Gap. Road ahead is posted "No Trespassing." *This is easy to miss.*

7.57—Cross very gullied old road. Ascend steeply.

8.06—Reach ridge crest.

8.64—Descend with rocky footing.

8.79—Ascend very steeply with rocky knoll on right.

8.86—Level. Good winter view from rocky crest on left.

9.18—Ascend.

9.55—Except for one small rise, the Trail ahead descends a side ridge with rocky footing.

10.15—Cross telephone line and turn right onto old road. On left, parallelling the road, is Devils Racecourse. This ancient stream deposit of boulders (with a small stream still beneath them) is similar to the Devils Racecourse in Maryland Trail Section 1, which has larger boulders.

10.28—Turn left off road and cross Devils Racecourse. (Straight ahead, road passes *Sand Spring,* on right, in 0.04 mi. To return, turn left onto intersecting road, cross Devils Racecourse, and rejoin *AT* in another 0.07 mi.)

10.33—Turn left onto old road and ascend steeply. On right, *Sand Spring* loop rejoins *AT.*

10.62—Go right at fork and descend through red maple, chestnut oak, sassafras, laurel, dogwood, and chestnut shoots. (To left, road leads 0.52 mi. to parking on Va-601.)

10.87—Crescent Rock. Excellent view of the Shenandoah River and Valley. The distinctive sloping terminus of the Massanutten Mountains can be seen in the distance. (From Crescent Rock, a path leads west along the cliff about 100 feet to a point where the cliff can be descended. By walking back, along the base of the cliff, to the foot of Crescent Rock, one can see the geological fold that forms a crescent in the rock. The core of the fold has been broken out by the action of ice in the crevices, forming a six-foot deep, arch-shaped indentation in the cliff. Pulpit Rock, or the "pinnacle," stands about 150 feet west of Crescent Rock. It is a column of rock that is separated from the cliff by a gap of about 10 feet. *The danger of snakes makes it inadvisable to descend the cliff during warm weather.*)

10.91—Old *AT* route intersects on right. Ahead, begin very steep, 500-foot descent. *Slippery at all times.*

11.24—Go left at fork. Blue-blazed trail on right leads 0.03 mi. to *spring,* passes a less desirable *spring,* and rejoins *AT* after 0.06 mi.

11.28—Blue-blazed trail rejoins on right. Go straight. Norway maples here. In a few more feet, go right at fork and cross rocky creek bed.

11.31—Ascend steeply through yellow poplars.

11.39—Bear right and ascend very steeply at first, then more easily, on rocky hillside. *Watch for poison ivy.*

11.70—Level. Descend ahead.

11.78—Good view of Shenandoah Valley from quartzite outcrop on right. Descend very steeply through black tupelo (blackgum), laurel, azaleas, and pine.

12.15—Level. Young oaks; older pines.

12.35—Begin general descent.

12.65—Go straight at crossing with path. Descend steeply.

12.69—Cross stream in Pigeon Hollow. Ahead, ascend gradually, then very steeply at times, by long switchbacks through rocks.

12.87—Fine view of Valley from rock outcrop. Trail undulates ahead, sometimes steeply.

13.42—Turn left onto Va-679.

13.45—Post with *AT* sign in median strip of Va-7, slightly west of Snickers Gap. (Bluemont is 0.8 mi. east of the gap.) To continue on the Trail, turn left and follow Va-7 east.

Detailed Trail Data—South to North

0—Post with *AT* sign in median strip of Va-7, slightly west of Snickers Gap. Follow Va-679 north.

0.03—Turn right off road and ascend steeply into woods. Trail undulates ahead, sometimes steeply, through laurel, pine, and chestnut oak.

0.58—Fine view of Valley from rock outcrop. Descend ahead, sometimes steeply, by long switchbacks through rocks.

0.76—Cross stream in Pigeon Hollow. Ascend steeply.

0.80—Go straight at crossing with path.

1.10—Level. Young oaks; older pines.

1.30—Ascend gradually at first, then very steeply, through laurel, azaleas, pine, and black tupelo (blackgum).

1.67—Good view of Shenandoah Valley from quartzite outcrop on left.

1.75—Descend gradually at first, then very steeply through rocks. *Watch for poison ivy.*

2.06—Bear left and descend steeply through yellow poplar forest.

2.16—Bear left and cross rocky creek bed.

2.17—Pass path that intersects on right, and then bear right at fork. Blue-blazed trail on left leads past a poor spring, to a better *spring* in 0.03 mi., and rejoins *AT* after 0.06 mi. Norway maples here.

2.21—Blue-blazed trail rejoins *AT* on left. Begin 500-foot ascent gradually at first, then very steeply. *Slippery at all times.*

2.54—Bear right at fork.

2.58—Crescent Rock. Excellent view of the Shenandoah River and Valley. The distinctive sloping terminus of the Massanutten Mountains can be seen in the distance. (From Crescent Rock, a path leads west along the cliff about 100 feet to a point where the cliff can be descended. Then by walking back, along the base of the cliff, to the foot of Crescent Rock, one can see the geological fold that forms a crescent in the rock. The core of the fold has been broken out by the action of ice in the crevices, forming a six-foot deep, arch-shaped indentation in the cliff. Pulpit Rock, or the "pinnacle," stands about 150 feet west of Crescent Rock. It is a column of rock that is separated from the cliff by a gap of about 10 feet. *The danger of snakes makes it inadvisable to descend the cliff during warm weather.*) Ascend through red maple, dogwood, laurel, oak.

2.83—Bear left at junction with old road. (To right, road leads 0.52 mi. to parking on Va-601.) Descend steeply ahead.

3.12—Go right at fork, leaving old road, and cross Devils Racecourse. This ancient stream deposit of boulders (with a small stream still beneath them) is similar to the Devils Racecourse in Maryland Section 1, which has larger boulders. (Straight ahead, road leads to *Sand Spring* in 0.07 mi. Turn right at junction; *spring* is on left a short distance beyond. To return, continue up road and rejoin *AT* in another 0.04 mi.)

3.17—Turn right onto old road and ascend. On left, *Sand Spring* loop rejoins *AT.*

3.30—Turn left, off road and onto path, cross telephone line, and ascend steeply with rocky footing.

3.90—Descend, rejoining main ridge.

4.27—Level. Ahead, good winter view from rocky crest.

4.59—Descend very steeply with rocky knoll on left.

4.66—Ascend.

4.81—Reach ridge crest.

5.39—Descend steeply.

5.88—Cross gullied old road and ascend steeply.

6.02—Bear left onto road in Wilson Gap. To right, road is posted "No Trespassing."

6.28—Path leads left to winter view from rocks. Ascend more gradually ahead.

6.59—Continue straight ahead, leaving road. (Short distance to left, road ends at clearing with good view.)

6.62—Pass The Lookout, an unusual pile of boulders on right. This once offered a view, hence the name, but trees have now completely blocked the view.

7.04—Blue-blazed trail on right descends steeply 0.27 mi. to Blackburn Trail Center. *Water* is available (not dependable in winter) from the Center.

7.27—Blue-blazed trail on right descends very steeply to campground (left fork in 0.11 mi.) and to Blackburn Center, in 0.28 mi.

7.36—Quartzite cliff on left offers good view.

8.15—The misnamed "Laurel Swamp." Path leads left to walled-in *Laurel Spring,* which is often dry.

8.20—Beautiful, profuse growth of periwinkle covers former house site on left. Rock walls outline yard, and slight chimney ruins are visible. Garden terraces rise above the site. Ascend.

8.30—Descend along eastern side of ridge crest.

8.60—Ascend.

8.91—Turn left onto old Shannondale Road, then turn right off road just ahead. (The road once connected Hillsboro to Shannondale Springs, a famous 19th-century resort that was patronized by Presidents.)

9.22—Level.

9.39—Descend generally, with rocky footing. Just ahead, on right, is The Deer Lick, a mossy area not visible from the Trail.

9.77—Ascend steeply.

9.89—Unblazed path leads left 0.08 mi. to Buzzard Rocks. (Path forks. Right branch leads to scree with no view. Left branch leads to Buzzard Rocks, with excellent view of Shenandoah River and Shannondale Lake. Good site for one tent near view.) Descend steeply.

10.14—Ascend.

10.27—Pass what appears to be a small remnant of a chimney, a few yards to left. Slight eastward view just ahead. Farther ahead, make short, very steep, descent.

10.45—Bear left onto old road. Ascend through very young forest on western side of ridge crest.

11.31—Winter view to east. Descend steeply ahead.

11.44—Bear right onto old road, then go left at fork just ahead. (Up hill to left, road leads 70 yards to excellent view from cleared crest near CATV tower.)

11.73—Old road intersects on right. Go straight.

11.79—Go left at fork and cross old road just ahead.

11.87—Old road intersects on left. Bear right.

12.33—Old road intersects on left. Bear right.

12.78—Go right at fork.

13.33—Stock pond in field on right. Former spring on right is polluted. Blue-blazed trail leads left 0.04 mi. to Keys Gap Shelter.

13.45—WVa-9 in Keys Gap. (There is a grocery store with *water* and telephone beside a gas station on WVa-9, a short distance to left. Another store is to right.) To continue on the Trail, cross WVa-9.

Blackburn Trail Center

SECTION 3
SNICKERS GAP TO ASHBY GAP
Distance 13.75 Miles

Road Approaches and Parking

Snickers Gap: This is on Va–7. The *AT* crosses Va–7 slightly west of the gap. There is room for several cars to park at the old rock crushers, on the southwest corner of Va–7 and Va–601. From Snickers Gap, Bluemont is 0.8 of a mile east, and Washington, D.C., is about 52 miles east.

To reach Va–605: Take Va–601 south from Snickers Gap, or north from Ashby Gap, and turn onto Va–605, a driveable dirt road, at Mt. Weather. There is room for a couple cars to park on the powerline right-of-way, at the *AT* crossing, about 1.4 miles west of Va–601.

Ashby Gap: This is on US–50. The *AT* crosses US–50 slightly west of the gap. The restaurant at the gap often allows one or two cars to park there, if permission is asked. There is also room for two cars to park on the shoulder of Va–600, at the junction with US–50 (south side of divided highway). A short access trail leads from here to the *AT*. Paris is 0.9 of a mile east, and Washington, D.C., is 56 miles east.

Points of Interest

There are excellent views from Bears Den Rocks (at 0.61/3.14 mi.) and Lookout Point (at 3.05/10.70 mi.). The dark and cool Fent Wiley Hollow (at 4.25/9.50 mi.) has a great variety of mature timber. The Trail also passes a former cabin site (at 5.47/8.28 mi.)

Maps

PATC Map #8 and USGS Bluemont and Paris Quadrangles

Shelter

Rod Hollow Shelter (0.12 mi. by side trail, at 10.25/3.50 mi.) accommodates seven persons. It has a *spring*, privy, and a sheltered picnic table and hearth.

Public Accommodations

Bears Den American Youth Hostel (0.16 mi. by side trail, at 0.61/13.14 mi.) has 20 bunks, toilets, showers, washer, dryer, cooking facilities, and telephone. No food is provided, but the hostel does sell soft drinks and snacks. The hostel opens at 5:00 p.m., all year, but the caretaker, if available, will allow *AT* thru-hikers to shower and do laundry during the day. Nightly fees per person are $9 for members of AYH, ATC, or PATC; $12 for others; $4 to sleep in yard (with use of facilities). Washer, dryer, and showers cost $1 each. Hikers may take *water* during the day from a tap on the left side of the house entrance, but must be sure to *turn it off.*

There is a restaurant on US–50 at Ashby Gap.

Supplies

There is a post office in Bluemont (0.8 mi. east of Snickers Gap), which has a General Delivery mail-drop that can be used by hikers. The Hostel (see above) has a telephone.

Water is available at the Bears Den Hostel (see above), and from *springs* at 0.90/12.85 mi., at 3.50/10.25 mi. (intermittent), at 5.50/8.25 mi., and at Rod Hollow Shelter.

Brief Description

Land closings have forced the *AT* off the main ridge in this section, but the Trail now follows a stable route on a protected corridor to the west. Consequently, the Trail seesaws in and out of a succession of hollows and over numerous side-ridges, making this probably the most difficult section in this book. *(Poison ivy* may be a problem in some areas.) Nevertheless, the route may be seen as an interesting contrast to the ridge-walking that dominates most of the *AT* route in Maryland and northern Virginia.

Side Trails

To Bears Den Hostel (at 0.61/13.14 mi.)
To *spring* (at 0.90/12.85 mi.)
To *Sawmill Spring* (at 3.50/10.25 mi.)

To Rod Hollow Shelter (at 10.25/3.50 mi.)
To Myron Glaser Cabin (at 12.02/1.73 mi.)

Detailed Trail Data—North to South

0—Post with *AT* sign in median strip of Va-7, slightly west of Snickers Gap. Go east on Va-7. (Bluemont is 0.8 mi. east of the gap.)

0.11—Turn right off Va-7 and onto graveled driveway, which narrows to a path almost immediately. Ascend generally, through dogwood, yellow poplar, oak, laurel, and sassafras.

0.61—Bears Den Rocks on right has outstanding view of Shenandoah Valley. (Path on left leads 0.16 mi. to Bears Den Hostel. Go left at road. *Tap water available.*)

0.65—Descend, steeply at times, through pines.

0.90—Blue-blazed trail on left leads 0.07 mi. to *spring.*

1.20—Cross creek on footbridge, then another stream just ahead. Pines end.

1.22—Cross old road. Ahead, Trail undulates through hickory, maple, and chestnut oak.

2.01—Descend very steeply, then more gradually.

2.32—Cross Spout Run, in deep, narrow ravine. Ahead, cross badly eroded, old road and ascend very steeply.

2.79—Nearly level ridge crest. Sparsely wooded, with low weeds. Watch for *poison ivy* for the next mile.

2.95—Peak of ridge.

3.05—Lookout Point, on left, has excellent view of mountains to south. Possible campsite. Descend steeply.

3.42—Cross old road.

3.49—Cross another branch of Spout Run.

3.50—Blue-blazed trail on left leads 0.05 mi. to intermittent *Sawmill Spring.* Ascend very steeply.

3.79—Top of Tomblin Hill.

3.88—Descend through an extensive area of ant mounds. *Don't stop here,* for ants cover the Trail as well.

4.05—Descend steeply.

4.25—Cross old road in Fent Wiley Hollow, a broad, dark hollow with a great variety of mature trees. Machine parts here, probably from an old vehicle.

4.30—Cross creek with two streams. Ahead, cross old road and pass old still site (in woods to left), and ascend.

4.39—Top of small ridge that divides the hollow. Descend and cross three streams ahead.

4.51—Turn right onto old road and ascend, very steeply at times.

4.96—Just below the rocky summit of Buzzard Hill. No view in summer. Descend, very steeply in one place ahead.

5.21—Turn right onto dirt road still in use. Ascend ahead.

5.44—Fork to right, off road and onto path, just after curve in road. *Easy to miss.* Level.

5.47—Pass ruined foundation of an old cabin on right.

5.50—*Spring* on left, beside Trail.

5.79—Turn right and descend very steeply with rocky footing on a recent relocation.

5.89—Cross creek in Reservoir Hollow.

6.04—Ascend steeply, then gradually, through many beeches.

6.25—Cross old, faint road.

6.46—Level, then descend ahead.

6.68—Leave woods. Bear left and cross Va-605. (Mt. Weather, on Va-601, is about 1.4 mi. to left.)

6.70—Enter woods. Descend steeply, then more gradually.

6.96—Pass through outcrops. Slight southward view from rocks.

7.13—Cross Morgan Mill Stream in Ashby Hollow. Hemlocks. Ahead, cross dirt road still in use and ascend, very steeply at times, through chestnut oak and pine.

7.92—Knoll on Piney Ridge. Descend steeply.

7.96—Ascend.

8.02—Descend, very steeply at times, from crest of ridge. Just ahead, turn left at confusing place in open forest.

8.56—Cross creek in Bolden Hollow and bear left onto old road at junction.

8.64—Turn right onto intersecting old road. Ascend, steeply at times.

8.78—Cross old road. Then turn left, off path and onto old road, just ahead.

8.88—Turn right off road and onto intersecting path.

9.09—Narrow ridge crest. Level ahead. *Watch for poison ivy and poison sumac.*

9.30—Descend, steeply at times, passing through rock outcrops ahead.

9.84—Cross old Transmountain Road in Rod Hollow. Level.

9.90—Cross stream. Ahead, cross another stream.

10.03—Ascend generally. Yellow poplars and saplings.

10.25—Blue-blazed trail on right leads 0.12 mi. to Rod Hollow Shelter and *spring*. Level. Ahead, cross two streams.

10.32—Cross old road. Ahead, ascend past old mine pits on both sides of Trail.

10.58—Level, then descends generally ahead.

10.69—Cross old stone wall.

10.91—Cross old road.

10.97—Shagbark hickory on right. Descend steeply past beeches.

11.04—Cross old stone wall.

11.06—Cross creek and stream in Duke Hollow and ascend through yellow poplar forest.

11.37—Descend through open forest of dogwood, pine, and yellow poplar saplings. Possible campsite.

11.55—Pass path that intersects on right. Trail undulates ahead.

11.86—Cross creek.

12.02—Blue-blazed trail on right leads to Myron Glaser Cabin, reserved for PATC members only.

12.24—Cross old road.

12.40—Cross creek.

12.91—Cross old road.

13.00—Cross underground telephone-cable right-of-way.

13.32—Pass old road that intersects on left. Young forest of beech, maple, hickory, elm, and lots of dogwood ahead.

13.65—Cross stream.

13.73—Leave woods. Cross US-50 bearing slightly right.

13.75—Dead tree with blaze in median strip of US-50, slightly west of Ashby Gap. (There is a restaurant and gas station at the gap.) To continue on the Trail, cross US-50 bearing slightly right and take path into woods.

Detailed Trail Data—South to North

0—Dead tree with blaze in median strip of US-50, slightly west of Ashby Gap. Cross US-50 bearing slightly right. (There is a restaurant and gas station at the gap.)

0.2—Enter woods and ascend through dense undergrowth, elms, and lots of dogwood.

0.10—Cross stream. Trail undulates ahead through young forest of beech, maple, hickory, and oak.

0.43—Go left at fork with old road.

0.75—Cross underground telephone-cable right-of-way.

0.84—Cross old road.

1.35—Cross creek.

1.51—Cross old road.

1.73—Blue-blazed trail on left leads to Myron Glaser Cabin, reserved for PATC members only.

1.89—Cross creek.

2.20—Bear right past path that intersects on left. Ascend through open forest of dogwood, pine, and yellow poplar saplings. Possible campsite ahead.

2.38—Open forest ends. Descend through yellow poplar forest.

2.67—Cross stream and creek in Duke Hollow.

2.71—Cross old stone wall. Ascend steeply past beeches.

2.78—Shagbark hickory on left. Descend, then ascend ahead.

2.84—Cross old road.

3.06—Cross old stone wall.

3.17—Descend past old mine pits on both sides of Trail.

3.43—Cross old road. Level. Ahead, cross two streams in Rod Hollow.

3.50—Go right at fork. Blue-blazed trail on left leads 0.12 mi. to Rod Hollow Shelter and *spring*. Descend generally.

3.72—Level.

3.80—Cross stream. Ahead, cross another stream.

3.91—Cross old Transmountain Road and ascend, steeply at times, passing through rock outcrops ahead.

4.45—Reach top of ridge. *Watch for poison ivy and poison sumac ahead.*

4.58—Descend, very steeply at times, along narrow ridge crest.

4.87—Turn left onto old road at junction.

4.96—Turn right off road and onto path. Cross old road ahead.

5.11—Turn left onto old road at junction in Bolden Hollow. Level.

5.18—Bear right, off road and onto path, and cross creek. Ahead, ascend very steeply.

5.70—Turn right and ascend at confusing place in open forest. Ahead, reach crest of Piney Ridge.

5.83—Knoll on Piney Ridge. Descend, very steeply at times, through pine and chestnut oak.

6.61—Cross dirt road still in use in Ashby Hollow. Ahead, cross Morgan Mill Stream and ascend. Hemlocks.

6.79—Pass through outcrops. Slight southward view from rocks. Ascend gradually ahead, then steeply.

7.05—Cross Va-605, bear left, and cross powerline right-of-way. (Mt. Weather, on Va-601, is about 1.4 mi. to right.)

7.07—Enter woods and ascend.

7.29—Descend gradually, then steeply, through many beeches.

7.50—Cross old, faint road.

7.71—Level, then ascend ahead.

7.86—Cross creek in Reservoir Hollow. Ascend very steeply.

7.96—Turn left at junction with former *AT* route. Level.

8.25—*Spring* on right, beside Trail.

8.28—Pass ruined foundation of old cabin on left.

8.31—Bear left at junction onto dirt road still in use. Descend.

8.54—Turn left off road and onto intersecting path. Ahead, ascend gradually, then very steeply.

8.79—Just below the rocky summit of Buzzard Hill. No view in summer. Descend, very steeply at times.

9.24—Turn left off road and onto intersecting path. Ahead, cross three streams in Fent Wiley Hollow and ascend.

9.36—Top of small ridge that divides hollow. Descend into broad, dark hollow with a great variety of mature trees.

9.40—Level. Ahead, pass old still site (in woods to right) and cross old road.

9.45—Cross creek with two streams.

9.50—Cross old road. Machine parts here, probably from an old vehicle. Ascend steeply.

9.70—Ascend more gradually. Ahead, pass through extensive area of ant mounds. *Don't stop here,* for ants cover the Trail as well.

9.87—Top of Tomblin Hill. Watch for *poison ivy* for the next mile.

9.96—Descend very steeply.

10.25—Blue-blazed trail on right leads 0.05 mi. to intermittent *Sawmill Spring.*

10.26—Cross a branch of Spout Run. Ascend steeply.

10.33—Cross old road.

10.70—Lookout Point, on right, has excellent view of mountains to south. Ridge is sparsely wooded, with low weeds, ahead. Possible campsite.

10.80—Peak of ridge.

10.96—Descend very steeply.

11.37—Cross badly eroded, old road.

11.43—Cross Spout Run, in deep, narrow ravine. Ascend gradually ahead, then very steeply.

11.74—Trail undulates ahead through hickory, maple, and chestnut oak.

12.53—Cross old road.

12.54—Cross stream, and then cross creek on footbridge. Ascend ahead, steeply at times, through pines.

12.85—Blue-blazed trail on right leads 0.07 mi. to *spring.*

13.14—Bears Den Rocks on left has outstanding view of Shenandoah Valley. (Path on right leads 0.16 mi. to Bears Den Hostel. Go left at road. *Tap water available.*) Ahead, descend generally, through oak, laurel, sassafras, yellow poplar, and dogwood.

13.64—Cross to median strip of Va-7 and turn left.

13.75—Post with *AT* sign in median strip of Va-7, slightly west of Snickers Gap. (Bluemont is 0.8 mi. east of the gap.) To continue on the Trail, follow Va-679 north.

SECTION 4
ASHBY GAP TO MANASSAS GAP
Distance 12.50 Miles

Road Approaches and Parking

Ashby Gap: This is on US-50. The *AT* crosses US-50 slightly west of the gap. The restaurant at the gap often allows one or two cars to park there, if permission is asked. There is also room for two cars to park on the shoulder of Va-600, at the junction with US-50 (south side of divided highway). A short access trail leads from here to the *AT*. Paris is 0.9 of a mile east, and Washington, D.C., is 56 miles east.

To reach Trico Tower Trail: From Va-55, at Manassas Gap, take Va-638 north for about five miles. There is room to park on the shoulder near the tower's access road. From the tower, a blue-blazed trail leads south 0.44 mi. to the *AT* (at 8.10/4.40 mi.), providing access for shorter hikes in this section.

To reach G. Richard Thompson State Wildlife Management Area Parking: From Va-55, at Manassas Gap, take Va-638 north to Parking Area #4, on right. Blue-blazed Ted Lake Trail follows old road 0.83 mi. from here to *AT* (at 10.12/2.38 mi.). Farther north on Va-638, Parking Area #7 lies on the right at junction with Blue Mountain Road. A gated old road leads right (east) 0.22 mi. from here to *AT* (at 6.76/5.74 mi.). There is another parking area near the *AT* on Signal Knob, but the road to it is not driveable for most cars.

To reach Sky Meadows State Park: See chapter on "Side Trails."

Manassas Gap: This is on Va-55, at Linden. The *AT* crosses Va-55 about a mile east of Linden, at the junction with Va-725. From the east, on I-66, exit onto Va-55 at Markham. From the west, on I-66, exit onto Va-55 at the Linden exit. The *AT*, going north, follows Va-725. There is room for several cars to park by the junction. Markham is about 3.4 miles east, Front Royal is about 7.1 miles west, and Washington, D.C., is 65 miles away.

Points of Interest

This section has an excellent view from a cleared slope (at 4.09/8.41 mi.) and interesting rock outcrops (at 10.79/1.71 mi.).

The Trico Firetower vicinity (0.44 mi. by side trail, at 8.10/4.40 mi.) is noted for its profuse growth of trillium.

Maps

PATC Map #8 and USGS Paris, Upperville, and Linden Quadrangles

Shelters and Campgrounds

Sky Meadows State Park (1.30 mi. by side trail, at 3.11/9.39 mi.) has camping at designated sites and a shelter. Nightly fee per campsite (limited to six persons per site) is $6. See chapter on "Side Trails."

Dick's Dome Shelter (0.18 mi. by side trail, at 5.40/7.10 mi.), beside Whiskey Hollow Creek, accommodates four. Privy on hillside, a short distance above. Taking water from the creek is not advisable. PATC member Dick George built this shelter on private land for *AT* hikers.

Manassas Gap Shelter (0.04 mi. by side trail, at 10.08/2.42 mi.) accommodates six persons and has a *spring* nearby.

Public Accommodations

There is a restaurant on US-50 at Ashby Gap.

Supplies

A post office, small store, and telephone are at the junction of Va-55 and Va-638, at Manassas Gap (Linden).

Water is available from *springs* at 4.36/8.14 mi. and at Manassas Gap Shelter, and from Sky Meadows State Park.

Brief Description

As in Virginia Section 3, the *AT* in this section has been relocated onto publicly acquired land in recent years. As a consequence of these relocations, and because a road follows the ridge crest, the Trail now snakes along the slopes, dipping in and out of numerous ravines. Although the footing is generally good, these undulations make this a moderately difficult day-hike.

Except for an outstanding view and odd rock formation, this section has no features of particular interest. There is, however, a great variety of flora: orchards, sapling forests, jungles of vines, and lots of wildflowers.

Much of the land in this section is part of the G. Richard Thompson Wildlife Management Area, which is under the jurisdiction of the Virginia Commission of Game and Inland Fisheries. Hunters may pose a danger during season.

Side Trails

To Sky Meadows State Park (at 3.11/9.39 mi.)
Dick's Dome Shelter (at 5.40/7.10 mi.)
Trico Tower Trail (at 8.10/4.40 mi.)
To Manassas Gap Shelter (at 10.08/2.42 mi.)
Ted Lake Trail (at 10.12/2.38 mi.)

Detailed Trail Data—North to South

0—Dead tree with blaze in median strip of US-50, slightly west of Ashby Gap. Cross US-50 bearing slightly right. (There is a restaurant and gas station at the gap.)

0.02—Enter woods on path. Cross stone wall and turn right onto old road with high grass. A sign says that George Washington once passed here.

0.16—Trail turns sharply left and ascends.

0.25—Access trail leads right 60 yards to parking at junction of Va-600 and US-50. Ahead, ascend through profuse dogwood followed by a dense tangle of vines.

0.72—Pass rock piles on left, in former cleared field. Good campsite.

0.86—Cross telephone cable right-of-way.

1.18—Turn right onto old road.

1.22—Turn left at crossroads and ascend steeply. Graveled road is posted "No Trespassing."

1.29—Turn right, off road and onto path, just before reaching gate. Descend ahead on a 50-foot-wide corridor of public land. *Stay on Trail.* The owner of the adjacent land often patrols the private, parallel road.

1.68—Turn right onto dirt road.

1.81—Turn left onto grassy road and ascend steeply. Interesting growth, with lots of locust trees.

2.04—Turn right at crossroads in grassy clearing.

2.10—Turn right, off road and onto path.

2.36—Rejoin old road, bearing right, and descend.

2.49—Turn left and ascend by a few long switchbacks.

2.69—Cross old road.

2.83—Turn right onto former fire-road and cross gas pipeline right-of-way. Good westward view.

2.86—Turn left, off road and onto path that parallels the pipeline corridor. *Easy to miss.* Trail enters Sky Meadows State Park.

2.98—Generally level Trail bears away from pipeline corridor and passes through dense growth of saplings.

3.11—Blue-blazed trail on left leads 1.73 mi. to Sky Meadows State Park Visitors Center, or 1.30 mi. to Park campground. See chapter on "Side Trails."

3.34—Enter the G. Richard Thompson State Wildlife Management Area. The *AT* passes through the Area for most of the next 7.26 miles. Hunters may pose a danger during season. Path intersects on right, but leads nowhere. Descend ahead.

3.85—Ascend.

4.09—Enter large clearing with low growth of sumac. Excellent view to south and southeast.

4.21—Old road leads right a short distance to parking area on Signal Knob. (Signal Knob was the site of a Civil War signal station. There is a soldier's cemetery on the eastern slope of the ridge.) Bear left and descend.

4.30—Enter woods.

4.36—Pass *spring* on left. Road has a pleasant canopy of shrubs.

4.86—Turn right, off road and onto path, leaving Game Commission land and entering land purchased for the Trail by the State of Virginia. Descend steeply.

5.26—Cross wide dirt road.

5.36—Cross creek in Whiskey Hollow.

5.40—Blue-blazed trail on left leads 0.18 mi. to Dick's Dome Shelter. Ascend steeply by switchbacks, re-entering Game Commission land.

5.55—Turn right onto old road.

5.64—Go left at fork.

5.99—Pass lone boulder and ascend more moderately.

6.47—Reach level crest.

6.61—Go left at fork off road and descend.

6.75—Turn left onto old road.

6.76—Cross old road in clearing. (To right, road leads 0.22 mi. to Parking Area #7.)

7.21—Bear right where abandoned, yellow-blazed trail intersects on left. Ahead, ascend very steeply, then more gradually.

7.74—Turn left onto dirt road, then almost immediately turn right off road and ascend very steeply. (To right, road leads 0.69 mi. to Va-638, just south of Trico Firetower.)

7.93—Cross old road.

8.10—Level. Blue-blazed Trico Tower Trail leads right 0.44 mi. to Trico (Tri-County) Firetower. (Built by the CCC in 1934, the 70-foot tower stands, at 2,207 feet, on the highest point in this section. *The tower should not be climbed.* The surrounding trees have now grown so high that no view is available except from the highest levels, and the decaying condition of the wooden stairs renders them extremely dangerous.)

8.77—Cross intermittent stream and ascend ahead.

9.19—Turn left onto dirt road. (Road leads right 0.42 mi. to Va-638.)

9.24—Turn right off road.

9.63—Descend steeply.

9.92—Bear right onto old road.

10.08—Pass chimney ruins on left. Blue-blazed trail leads left 0.04 mi. to Manassas Gap Shelter and *spring*.

10.12—Turn left at crossroads. (To right, the Game Commission's blue-blazed Ted Lake Trail leads 0.83 mi. to Parking Area #4.)

10.14—Go straight as blue-blazed Ted Lake Trail goes left. Ascend through hickory, sassafras, oak, yellow poplar.

10.32—Turn right, off road and onto path, at edge of small, game clearing. *Easy to miss.* Trail undulates ahead around right side of knob.

10.60—Leave G. Richard Thompson Wildlife Management Area. Descend, passing dense undergrowth and dogwood.

10.79—Interesting rock formations. Monolithic outcrops jut up from the ground.

10.98—Old wall on left.

11.08—Turn left onto old road.

11.09—Go right at fork, off road and onto path. Forest becomes more open.

11.24—Turn left at intersection. Ascend.

11.29—Go right at fork and descend, steeply at times. Northern red oak and chestnut predominate.

12.05—Bear to right of open area and then turn left onto mowed path along telephone line. Barbed wire fence parallels path on right. Sycamores.

12.14—Cross stile at edge of farm and turn left onto Va-725. (Private road to right; no trespassing.)

12.27—Pass private road on right.

12.50—Intersect Va-55 after passing under I-66 overpasses. (Linden, in Manassas Gap, is about 1 mi. to right on level route. It has a post office, small store, and telephone at junction with Va-638. Also at junction is Discovery Monument, commemorating the supposed site from which John Lederer first saw the Shenandoah Valley in 1670.) To continue on the Trail, cross Va-55 and enter woods to right of junction.

Detailed Trail Data—South to North

0—Junction of Va-55 and Va-725. Follow Va-725, passing under I-66 overpasses. (Linden, in Manassas Gap, is about 1 mi. to left on level route. It has a post office, small store, and telephone at junction with Va-638. Also at junction is Discovery Monument, commemorating the supposed site from which John Lederer first saw the Shenandoah Valley in 1670.)

0.23—Pass private road on left.

0.36—Where road is posted "No Trespassing," cross stile on right, beside driveway to white farmhouse. Then follow mowed path along telephone line, with barbed wire fence on left. Sycamores.

0.45—Turn right, leaving path along telephone line, and ascend into woods ahead, sometimes steeply. Northern red oak and chestnuts predominate.

1.21—Old road intersects on right. Go straight.

1.26—Go right at fork.

1.41—Old road intersects on right. Go straight. Old wall on right.

1.42—Turn right, off road and onto path.

1.71—Interesting rock formations. Monolithic outcrops jut up from ground.

1.90—Enter the G. Richard Thompson Wildlife Management Area. The *AT* passes through the Area for most of the next 7.26 mi. Hunters may pose a danger during season. Trail undulates ahead around left side of knob.

2.18—Turn left onto old road at edge of small, game clearing. Descend ahead through hickory, sassafras, oak, and yellow poplar.

2.36—Blue-blazed Ted Lake Trail intersects on right. Go straight.

2.38—Turn right at crossroads. (Blue-blazed Ted Lake Trail continues straight ahead 0.83 mi. to Parking Area #4.)

2.42—Blue-blazed trail leads right 0.04 mi. to Manassas Gap Shelter and *spring*. Pass chimney ruins on right and ascend steeply.

2.58—Bear left off road and onto path.

2.87—Level, then descend ahead.

3.26—Turn left onto dirt road.

3.31—Turn right off road and onto path. (Road continues 0.42 mi. to Va-638.)

3.73—Cross intermittent stream. Trail ascends, then becomes level ahead.

4.40—Blue-blazed Trico Tower Trail leads left 0.44 mi. to Trico (Tri-County) Firetower. (Built by the CCC in 1934, the 70-foot tower stands, at 2,207 feet, on the highest point in this section. *The tower should not be climbed.* The surrounding trees have now grown so high that no view is available except from the highest levels, and the decaying condition of the wooden stairs renders them extremely dangerous.) Descend very steeply.

4.57—Cross old road.

4.74—Turn left onto dirt road, then almost immediately turn right off road and descend. (To left, road leads 0.69 mi. to Va-638, just south of Trico Firetower.)

5.29—Bear left where abandoned, yellow-blazed trail intersects on right. Ascend.

5.74—Cross old road in clearing. (To left, road leads 0.22 mi. to Parking Area #7.)

5.75—Turn right off road and onto path.

5.89—Bear right onto old road. Level, then descend.

6.51—Pass lone boulder on right and descend very steeply.

6.86—Bear right onto intersecting old road.

6.95—Turn left off road and onto path.

7.10—Blue-blazed trail on right leads 0.18 mi. to Dick's Dome Shelter.

7.14—Cross creek in Whiskey Hollow, leaving Game Commission land and entering land purchased for the Trail by the State of Virginia. Ascend.

7.21—Cross wide dirt road.

7.64—Turn left onto old road, re-entering Game Commission land. Road has a pleasant canopy of shrubs ahead.

8.14—Pass *spring* on right.

8.20—Enter large clearing with low growth of sumac.

8.29—Old road leads a short distance to parking area on Signal Knob, maintained by the Game Commission. (Signal Knob was the site of a Civil War signal station. There is a soldiers' cemetery on the eastern slope of the knob.) Bear right, with excellent view to south and southeast.

8.41—Enter woods and descend on path.

8.65—Ascend.

9.16—Leave Game Commission land and enter Sky Meadows State Park. Pass path on left, which leads nowhere. Generally level ahead.

9.39—Blue-blazed trail on right leads 1.73 mi. to Sky Meadows State Park Visitor Center, or 1.30 mi. to Park campground. See chapter on "Side Trails." Ahead, Trail passes through dense growth of saplings.

9.52—Trail bears left and parallels gas pipeline right-of-way.

9.64—Turn right onto former fire-road, leaving Sky Meadows State Park, and cross pipeline corridor. Good westward view.

9.67—Turn left, off road and onto path, and descend. Do not attempt to short-cut on the fire-road, which is private property posted "No Trespassing." The landowner often patrols the road.

9.81—Cross old road.

10.01—Turn right onto road and ascend.

10.14—Bear left off road and onto path.

10.40—Bear left, rejoining old road, and descend steeply. Interesting growth, with lots of locust trees, ahead.

10.46—Turn left at crossroads in grassy clearing.

10.69—Turn right onto dirt road and ascend.

10.82—Turn left off road and onto path. This is a 50-foot-wide corridor of public land. *Stay on Trail.*

11.21—Turn left onto dirt road and descend steeply.

11.28—Turn right at crossroads and descend more gradually.

11.32—Turn left off road and onto path.

11.64—Cross telephone cable right-of-way.

11.78—Pass rock piles on right, in former cleared field. Descend ahead through a dense tangle of vines, then through profuse dogwood.

12.25—Access trail on left leads 60 yards to parking at junction of Va-600 and US-50.

12.34—Trail turns sharply right and ascends on old road with high grass. Ahead, a sign says that George Washington once passed here.

12.48—Turn left off road and cross stone wall. Then cross US-50, bearing slightly right, to median strip. (There is a restaurant and gas station at Ashby Gap, a short distance to right.)

12.50—Dead tree with blaze in median strip of US-50. To continue on the Trail, cross US-50 bearing slight right.

SECTION 5
MANASSAS GAP TO US-522
Distance 8.39 Miles

Road Approaches and Parking

Manassas Gap: This is on Va-55, at Linden. The *AT* crosses Va-55 about a mile east of Linden, at the junction with Va-725. From the east, on I-66, exit onto Va-55 at Markham. From the west, on I-66, get onto Va-55 at the Linden exit. The *AT*, going south, enters the woods just a few yards west of the junction. There is room for several cars to park by the junction. Markham is about 3.4 miles east, Front Royal is about 7.1 miles west, and Washington, D.C., is about 65 miles away.

Va-638: There is no parking near this crossing.

US-522: The *AT* crosses this highway at a point 1.5 miles west of Chester Gap and 3.2 miles east of Va-55, in Front Royal. Washington, D.C., via I-66 and Front Royal, is about 74 miles away. There is room for several cars to park on the south side of the highway at the *AT* crossing.

Points of Interest

The highlight of this section is an abandoned farm on top of a mountain with outstanding views in several directions (at 1.25/7.14 mi.).

Maps

PATC Map #8 and USGS Linden and Front Royal Quadrangles

Shelter and Campgrounds

The newly constructed Linden Shelter, campground (with tent platforms), picnic pavilion, privy, and nearby *spring* should be complete by the time this guide appears (0.03 mi. by side trail, at 3.12/5.27 mi.).

Mosby Campsite (0.06 mi. by side trail, at 4.97/3.42 mi.) has several places for tents and a nearby *spring*, but no other facilities.

Supplies

A post office, telephone, and small store are at the junction of Va-55 and Va-638, at Manassas Gap (Linden).

Water is available from a *spring* at 3.15/5.24 mi. and from *Tom Sealock Spring* (0.09 mi. by side trail, at 4.97/3.42 mi.).

Brief Description

From either direction, this section poses a nearly 1,000-foot ascent along the slopes of High Knob and a 600-foot ascent of a neighboring mountain. The ascents are somewhat steeper from the south. The footing is generally good. This section can be combined with Virginia Section 6 for a moderate day-hike, if hiked from south to north.

North to south: From Va-55, a mile east of Manassas Gap, the *AT* climbs 600 feet to an abandoned farm on top of a mountain and then descends 600 feet to Va-638. Next, the Trail ascends along a ridge, crosses some hollows to follow another ridge, and passes just above the saddle between High Knob and Ravensden Rock. The Trail zigzags steeply along the southern slope of High Knob, and then descends on an old road through the pleasant Bear Hollow. Before reaching US-522, the Trail briefly parallels the highway.

South to north: From US-522, the *AT* briefly parallels the highway before ascending the pleasant Bear Hollow on an old road. Then the Trail zigzags, sometimes steeply, on a path along the southern slope of High Knob. After passing slightly above a saddle between High Knob and Ravensden Rock, the Trail descends along a ridge and crosses some hollows to follow another ridge down to Va-638. Next, the Trail climbs 600 feet to an abandoned farm on top of a mountain and then descends 600 feet to Va-55, one mile east of Manassas Gap.

Side Trails

To Linden Shelter and campground (at 3.12/5.27 mi.)

To Mosby Campsite and *Tom Sealock Spring* (at 4.97/3.42 mi.)

Detailed Trail Data—North to South

0—Junction of Va-55 and Va-725. Enter woods through

weedy area to right of junction. Ahead, a small bulletin board, posted on tree on right, has Trail information; and a boardwalk crosses several channels of Goose Creek, with beaver dams and activity on right. (Linden, in Manassas Gap, is about 1 mi. to right on level route. It has a post office, small store, and telephone at junction with Va-638. Also at junction is Discovery Monument, commemorating the supposed site from which John Lederer first saw the Shenandoah Valley in 1670.)

0.12—Cross railroad tracks and ascend steeply.

0.38—Bear left around curve. Path intersects on right.

0.48—Cross faint old road.

0.49—Turn right onto old road at junction. Go left at fork in a few yards.

0.74—Switchback steeply to left at base of large cliff.

0.83—Switchback to right over boulders.

0.97—Cross stile.

1.04—Enter old orchard, part of abandoned farm on top of mountain. Go straight, with good view of High Knob. (The route shown on the 1985 Provisional Edition of PATC Map #8 is inaccurate. The Trail passes along the crest of the mountain.)

1.09—Turn right onto old, sunken road and follow *AT* posts toward abandoned farm buildings.

1.17—Pass between buildings, *which should not be entered.* Aim for peak of cleared hill ahead.

1.25—Excellent view down Trumbo Hollow from foundation on left. Cross center of field atop hill, bearing slightly right from the center to the next post. Superb view, through gap, of Shenandoah Valley and the West Virginia mountains beyond.

1.35—Leave clearing and descend. Ahead, cross stile and ascend.

1.46—Cross over crest of ridge, not along it, through an old field that is becoming overgrown. Descend ahead, with view of High Knob.

1.67—Turn right and descend on old road.

1.82—Bear left off road at edge of private farm. Go around left side of corral. Descend very steeply through pasture toward graveled farm road. *Stay on Trail.*

1.96—Cross stile at left of gate.

2.00—Turn left onto paved Va-638. *Watch for traffic.*

2.04—Turn right off road a few yards after driveway on left. Ahead, small bulletin board, posted on tree on right, has Trail information. Pass through overgrown field.

2.17—Cross bridge over small stream. Ascend, generally steeply. Ahead, Trail levels off as dense undergrowth replaces mature trees.

2.51—Go straight where another path forks to left in small clearing.

2.55—Turn right, leaving path that follows ridge crest. Trail undulates ahead, and mature trees return.

2.72—Cross old stone wall. Ascend ahead.

3.05—Old road intersects on right. Go straight.

3.12—Trail on right leads 0.03 mi. to recently constructed Linden Shelter and campground.

3.15—Go straight at crossroads. *Do not enter* ruined old house on right. A *spring* lies a few yards to left of house.

3.31—Turn right, off road and onto path, and descend briefly. Lots of hickory, including shagbark, and yellow poplar throughout area.

3.78—Base of small cliff.

4.26—Cross powerline right-of-way. Fair view to right. Ahead, pass through a very young forest dominated by dogwood. The lack of old trees suggests a former clear-cut.

4.64—Cross dirt road.

4.77—Cross old road. Ahead, cross old stone wall.

4.91—Cross old road.

4.97—Blue-blazed trail leads left 0.06 mi. to Mosby Campsite (primitive) and another 50 yards downhill to *Tom Sealock Spring* (named for one of Col. Mosby's men, who lived here after the Civil War). (The site is on ten acres of land donated to the PATC in 1965 by Mrs. Mary H. Keyser. PATC donated the land to the National Park Service in 1987. A former shelter on this site was apparently stolen in 1980 for the sake of its chestnut logs.)

5.01—Cross stream and ascend. Spotted touch-me-nots may be seen here.

5.12—Cross Fire-road 3460.

5.31—Turn right onto old road.

5.55—Turn left off road and descend very steeply with rocky footing.

5.71—Ascend steeply with rocky footing.

5.94—Descend steeply.

6.10—To end of section, National Park Service easement passes over land belonging to the Research and Conservation Center. (The Center is a 4,000-acre wildlife preserve belonging to the National Zoological Park, an agency of the Smithsonian Institution. The land was formerly a USDA livestock research station and, before that, a U.S. Cavalry remount post.) *Camping and hunting are prohibited.*

6.43—Go right at fork. Blue-blazed path on left is used for access by trail maintenance workers. Ahead, ticks are common.

6.55—Cross old road.

6.62—Turn right onto old road.

6.70—Turn left off road and onto path. Pass through area of dense undergrowth ahead.

7.03—Descend gradually.

7.62—Cross Bear Hollow Creek.

8.10—Just after gravel road intersects on right, turn right between the two fences. Trail undulates through scrub between fences, paralleling highway. View of Lake Front Royal across highway.

8.36—Turn left and almost immediately turn right.

8.39—US-522. To continue on the Trail, cross US-522.

Detailed Trail Data—South to North

0—US-522. Ascend embankment and parallel highway. For the first 2.29 mi., the Trail follows a National Park Service easement over land belonging to the Research and Conservation Center. (The Center is a 4,000-acre wildlife preserve belonging to the National Zoological Park, an agency of the Smithsonian Institution. The land was formerly a USDA livestock research station and, before that, a U.S. Cavalry remount post.) *Camping and hunting are prohibited.* Ticks are common in this area.

0.02—Turn left and almost immediately turn right. Pass through scrub ahead, with view of Lake Front Royal across highway.

0.29—Turn left onto gravel road, then bear right onto grassy old road, between fence and Bear Hollow Creek.

0.77—Cross creek.

1.36—Ascend steeply through area of dense undergrowth.

1.69—Turn right onto old road.

1.77—Turn left off road and onto path.

1.84—Cross old road.

1.96—Bear left. Blue-blazed trail on right is used for access by trail maintenance workers.

2.29—Trail leaves National Zoological Park land, but continues on National Park Service land.

2.45—Descend steeply.

2.68—Ascend very steeply with rocky footing.

2.84—Turn right onto road and descend.

3.08—Turn left off road and onto path.

3.27—Cross Fire-road 3460.

3.38—Cross stream. Spotted touch-me-knots may be seen here.

3.42—Go left at fork. Blue-blazed trail leads right 0.06 mi. to Mosby Campsite (primitive) and another 50 yards downhill to *Tom Sealock Spring* (named for one of Col. Mosby's men, who lived here after the Civil War). (The site is on ten acres of land donated to the PATC in 1965 by Mrs. Mary H. Keyser. PATC donated the land to the National Park Service in 1987. A former shelter on this site was apparently stolen in 1980 for the sake of its chestnut logs.)

3.48—Cross old road. Ahead, cross old stone wall.

3.62—Cross old road.

3.75—Cross dirt road. Ahead, pass through a very young forest dominated by dogwood. The lack of old trees suggests a former clear-cut.

4.13—Cross powerline right-of-way. Fair view to left.

4.52—Small cliff on left. Descend ahead through lots of hickory, including shagbark, and yellow poplar.

5.08—Turn left onto road.

5.24—Go straight at crossroads. *Do not enter* ruined old house on left. A *spring* lies a few yards to left of house.

5.27—Trail on left leads 0.03 mi. to recently constructed Linden Shelter and campground.

5.34—Go right at fork.

5.67—Cross old stone wall. Trail undulates ahead.

5.84—Turn left at junction. Dense undergrowth replaces mature trees. Descend ahead.

5.88—Trail intersects on right in small clearing. Go straight.

6.22—Cross bridge over small stream. Pass through overgrown field ahead.

6.35—Turn left onto paved Va-638. *Watch for traffic.* A small bulletin board, posted on tree on left just before turn, has Trail information.

6.39—Turn right off road and onto graveled farm road.

6.43—Cross stile at right of gate. Follow line of trees steeply up hill to right side of corral. This is a private farm; *stay on Trail.*

6.57—Turn right onto old road and ascend.

6.72—Turn left off road. Ahead, view of High Knob can be seen to rear.

6.93—Cross over crest of ridge, through an old field that is becoming overgrown. Descend and cross stile ahead.

7.04—Enter cleared field of abandoned farm on mountain top. Cross center of field and descend to abandoned farm building. Superb view on left, through gap, of Shenandoah Valley and the West Virginia mountains beyond. Ahead, excellent view down Trumbo Hollow from foundation on right. Follow *AT* posts. (The route shown on the 1985 Provisional Edition of PATC Map #8 is inaccurate. The Trail passes along the crest of the mountain.)

7.22—Pass between buildings, *which should not be entered.* Ascend sunken farm road ahead.

7.30—Turn left off road and cross old orchard.

7.35—Leave orchard and enter woods.

7.42—Cross stile and descend ahead over boulders.

7.56—Switchback to left and descend steeply.

7.65—Switchback to right at base of large cliff.

7.90—Go straight onto old road, which intersects from left, and then turn left, off road and onto path, in a few yards.

7.91—Cross faint old road.

8.01—Bear right around curve. Path intersects on left.

8.27—Cross railroad tracks. Ahead, a boardwalk crosses several channels of Goose Creek, with beaver dams and activity on left; and a small bulletin board, posted on tree on left near end of section, has Trail information.

8.39—Junction of Va-55 and Va-725. (Linden, in Manassas Gap, is about 1 mi. to left on level route. It has a post office, small store, and telephone at junction with Va-638. Also at junction is Discovery Monument, commemorating the supposed site from which John Lederer first saw the Shenandoah Valley in 1670.) To continue on the Trail, cross Va-55 and follow Va-725.

Hikers beware!

SECTION 6
US-522 TO SHENANDOAH NATIONAL PARK
Distance 3.84 Miles

Road Approaches and Parking

US-522: The *AT* crosses this highway at a point 1.5 miles west of Chester Gap and 3.2 miles east of Va-55, in Front Royal. Washington, D.C., via I-66 and Front Royal, is about 74 miles away. There is room for several cars to park on the south side of the highway.

To reach Va-602 and Va-601: From US-522, between Front Royal and the *AT* crossing, take paved Va-604 south. Graveled Va-602 forks to the left; room for two cars to park. Farther ahead on Va-604, graveled Va-601 forks to the left. Va-601 has a parking area (on PATC land) on the right, marked by a sign, with room for about four cars. A blue-blazed access trail, opposite, ascends 0.18 mi. to the *AT.*

To reach Shenandoah National Park boundary: From US-522, turn onto crescent road on south side of Chester Gap. Turn onto Va-610 and follow it to gate at Park boundary. There is room for several cars to park here. Continue on foot up dirt road (old Compton Gap Road) for 0.52 mi. Then turn right onto *AT* and descend (passing Possums Rest Trail, over which the *AT* will soon be rerouted) another 0.17 mi. to Park boundary, at southern end of Section 6.

Points of Interest

There are two good views (at 0.45/3.39 mi. and 1.62/2.17 mi.). The variety of growth is also interesting.

Maps

PATC Map #9 and USGS Front Royal and Chester Gap Quadrangles

Shelters

Tom Floyd Wayside (short distance by side trail, at 3.40/0.44 mi.) has shelter and a *spring*. Use is free on a first-come, first-served basis. *Camp fires and group camping are prohibited.* Users must carry out all trash.

Supplies

Water is available from *Ginger Spring* (0.15 mi. by side trail, at 3.28/0.56 mi.).

Brief Description

From north to south, this section has 1,600 feet of ascent and only 300 feet of descent. The footing is very good. This section can be combined with Virginia Section 5 for a moderate day-hike, if hiked from south to north.

North to south: From US-522, the *AT* crosses Sloan Creek and ascends beside a meadow to a saddle on a spur-ridge. Then the Trail descends into Harmony Hollow, crosses Moore Run, and ascends with a good view of the hollow. After passing some houses on Va-601, the Trail turns left and ascends by switchbacks to the Shenandoah National Park boundary.

South to north: From the Shenandoah National Park boundary, the *AT* descends by switchbacks into Harmony Hollow. After passing some houses on Va-601, the Trail turns right and continues to descend, passing a good view of the hollow. Then the Trail crosses Moore Run, ascends to a saddle on a spur-ridge, descends beside a meadow, and crosses Sloan Creek before reaching US-522.

Side Trails

Access trail from Va-601 (at 2.50/1.34 mi.)
To *Ginger Spring* (at 3.28/0.56 mi.)
To Tom Floyd Wayside (at 3.40/0.44 mi.)

Detailed Trail Data—North to South

0—US-522. Descend to creek. The Trail ahead follows a National Park Service easement over land belonging to the Research and Conservation Center. (The Center is a 4,000 acre wildlife preserve belonging to the National Zoological Park, an agency of the Smithsonian Institution. The land was formerly a USDA livestock research station and, before that, a U.S. Cavalry remount post.) *Camping and hunting are prohibited.*

0.04—Cross newly built footbridge over polluted Sloan Creek.

0.08—Cross footbridge over polluted marsh. Ascend with fenced meadow and good view on right. (A World War II prisoner-of-war camp was on top of the ridge above the former cavalry post.) Ticks are common in this area. Frequent inspections for ticks are recommended.

0.45—Enter woods dominated by yellow poplars (tuliptrees).

0.75—Just before crossing ditch, evening orchids may be seen beside large yellow poplar.

0.91—Cross saddle of spur-ridge. Descend steeply through mature beech-maple forest.

NOTE: Trail may be relocated between here and 3.20 mi.

1.38—Cross Va-602. (Enter land owned by Virginia Polytechnic Institute, part of which is being developed into a 4-H educational center.) Trail undulates ahead through forest where beech trees predominate.

1.41—Cross Moore Run. Do not take water from here, nor at the stream ahead, for there are houses up-stream.

1.51—Cross stream and ascend.

1.62—Pass through overgrown meadow, with good view of Harmony Hollow on right.

1.69—Cross telephone line and pass through area of dense undergrowth.

1.96—Descend steeply through open forest of walnut, yellow poplar, and sycamore.

2.08—Bear left where path of former *AT* route intersects on right. Ascend.

2.31—Cross stile by "private property" sign. The Trail leaves VPI land and enters the Harmony Hollow scenic easement area, the first such easement established in Virginia. Just ahead, the Trail briefly crosses PATC land. *Stay on Trail.*

2.50—Blue-blazed access trail leads right 0.18 mi. to parking area on Va-601. (Two rare chinquapin oak trees grow just off the side trail, about 100 feet from the *AT,* near rock outcrops.)

2.63—Turn right onto level, 19th century coach-road, leaving PATC land. Ahead, pass house (built in 1886) on left.

2.67—Cross small bridge over creek and turn left off road immediately after intersecting Va-601. Do not take water from here, for there are houses up-stream.

2.70—Cross rock causeway over creek. Ascend through extensive growth of white ash and yellow poplar. A strong aroma of sassafras may be detectable in places.

3.28—Blue-blazed trail leads right 0.15 mi. to *Ginger Spring*.

3.40—Path leads right to Tom Floyd Wayside. Oak and hickory predominate ahead.

3.84—Shenandoah National Park boundary. The *AT* continues to ascend (passing Possums Rest Trail, which leads right to a superb 160-degree overlook) for 0.17 mi. to junction with old Compton Gap Road. Trail turns right at junction. Parking at end of Va-610 is 0.52 mi. to left.

Detailed Trail Data—South to North

0—Shenandoah National Park boundary. Descend through an oak-hickory forest on the Harmony Hollow scenic easement, the first such easement established in Virginia.

0.44—Path leads left to Tom Floyd Wayside. Pass through extensive growth of white ash and yellow poplar (tuliptree) ahead.

0.56—Blue-blazed trail leads left 0.15 mi. to *Ginger Spring*. Ahead, a strong aroma of sassafras may be detectable in places.

NOTE: Trail may be relocated between 0.64 mi. and 2.94 mi.

1.14—Level. Cross rock causeway over creek. Do not take water from here, for there are houses up-stream. *Stay on Trail.*

1.17—Intersect Va-601 and immediately turn right onto 19th century coach-road. Cross small bridge over creek and pass house (built in 1886) on right.

1.21—Turn left off road and onto path. Enter PATC land and descend.

1.34—Blue-blazed access trail leads left 0.18 mi. to parking area on Va-601. (Two rare chinquapin oak trees grow just off the side trail, about 100 feet from the *AT,* near rock outcrops.)

1.53—Cross stile. Trail leaves Harmony Hollow scenic easement and enters a National Park Service easement over land owned by Virginia Polytechnic Institute, part of which is being developed into a 4-H educational center.

1.76—Bear right at fork with former *AT* route. Ascend steeply through open forest of walnut, yellow poplar, and sycamore.

1.88—Descend.

2.12—Pass through area of dense undergrowth and cross telephone line just ahead.

2.17—Pass through overgrown meadow, with good view of Harmony Hollow on left.

2.33—Cross stream. Do not take water from here, nor at the stream ahead, for there are houses up-stream. Trail undulates ahead through forest where beech trees predominate.

2.43—Cross Moore Run.

2.46—Cross Va-602. (Leave VPI land and enter land belonging to the Research and Conservation Center. The Center is a 4,000-acre wildlife preserve belonging to the National Zoological Park, an agency of the Smithsonian Institution. The land was formerly a USDA livestock research station and, before that, a U.S. Cavalry remount post.) *Camping and hunting are prohibited.* Ascend steeply through mature beech-maple forest.

2.93—Cross saddle of spur-ridge. Descend through forest dominated by yellow poplars.

3.09—Just after crossing ditch, evening orchids may be seen beside large yellow poplar.

3.39—Leave woods and descend with fenced meadow and good view on left. (A World War II prisoner-of-war camp was on top of the ridge above the former cavalry post.) Ticks are common in this area. Frequent inspections for ticks are recommended.

3.76—Cross footbridge over polluted marsh.

3.80—Cross newly built footbridge over polluted Sloan Creek.

3.84—US-522. To continue on the Trail, cross US-522 and ascend embankment.

CHAPTER 7
SIDE TRAILS

The PATC maintains a number of blue-blazed side trails that either intersect or parallel the *AT*. They are noted in the detailed Trail descriptions for each section. Most of these are short paths leading to shelters, or viewpoints, and do not require further description. The following trails, however, deserve a detailed description because of their particular features and/or the access to the *AT* that they provide.

The approximately 220-mile Tuscarora-Big Blue Trail provides a loop to the west of the *AT*. It intersects the *AT* at Blue Mountain, Pennsylvania, and in the northern section of Shenandoah National Park. Separate guidebooks to this trail have been published by the PATC and the Keystone Trails Association.

There are also numerous side trails in the Catoctin Mountains and in the Washington, D.C., suburbs, but these too are covered in separate guidebooks published by the PATC.

MARYLAND
DEVILS RACECOURSE SHELTER TRAIL
Distance 0.42 Miles

Cross-reference: Maryland Section 1

Access: From the *AT* crossing of Md-491 (Raven Rock Road), take Ft. Ritchie Road (sign says "Camp Ritchie Road") north for 0.8 of a mile. There is room for several cars to park on the left, beside the trailhead.

Detailed Trail Data—From Road

0—Ft. Ritchie Road. Descend old dirt road, which is blocked by a boulder. (This was originally part of the old Catoctin Trail, which formerly linked the *AT* to the Catoctin Mountains.)

0.06—Cross Devils Racecourse, an ancient stream deposit of boulders. This is much more interesting than its Virginia namesake because the boulders are bigger and the swath is more open. Ascend ahead.

0.13—Fork to left leads to shelter in 30 yards.

0.20—Pass *spring* on right. Ascend very steeply on badly eroded trail. Very slippery when wet, or when leaves are down. Poorly blazed; follow main gully.

0.36—Reach top of escarpment. Level.

0.42—Junction with *AT.* Pen Mar Road is 5.22 mi. to right. Md-491, in Raven Rock Hollow, is 1.10 mi. to left.

Detailed Trail Data—From AT

0—Junction with *AT.* (This was originally part of the old Catoctin Trail, which formerly linked the *AT* to the Catoctin Mountains.)

0.06—Descend very steeply on badly eroded trail. Very slippery when wet, or when the leaves are down. Poorly blazed; follow main gully.

0.22—Pass *spring* on left. Descend gradually ahead on old road and pass shelter on right.

0.36—Cross Devils Racecourse, an ancient stream deposit of boulders. This is much more interesting than its Virginia namesake because the boulders are bigger and the swath is more open. Ascend ahead.

0.42—Ft. Ritchie Road. Md-491, in Raven Rock Hollow, is 0.8 mi. to right.

BEAR SPRING CABIN TRAIL
Distance 1.04 Miles

Cross-reference: Maryland Section 5

Access: From US-Alt. 40, take Marker Road (or take Bolivar Road, or Reno Monument Road, to Marker Road) and turn onto Mountain Church Road. Turn right onto road beside Locust Valley First Church of God. Park in church parking lot in one of three designated spaces in the far corner, nearest the line of trees.

From US-340, take Md-17 north. Turn left onto Gapland Road, in Burkittsville. Then turn right onto Mountain Church Road and see above.

Detailed Trail Data—From Road

0—Junction beside church. Ascend road past house and trailer.

0.18—Pass pond on left, as road curves sharply to right.

0.34—Siding on right provides space for one car to park. Turn left off road and cross creek, reaching Bear Spring Cabin. From here, the trail forks. (Right fork, leading up hollow, is only half as long as left fork. It passes *Bear Spring* and rejoins the other fork in 0.19 mi.) Left fork leads briefly down hollow before circling back up.

0.41—Pass stone cellar of house, on left, in profuse growth of periwinkle.

0.45—Turn right onto old road.

0.49—Several old gullied roads intersect in a small area. *Follow blazes carefully.*

0.72—The other blue-blazed fork rejoins on right. *Bear Spring* is a few yards down this fork. Ascend more steeply ahead.

0.87—Bear left as Old Dug Road intersects on right. Just ahead, the White Rocks Trail (see below) intersects on right. Continue ahead on old road with good winter view.

1.04—Junction with *AT.*

Detailed Trail Data—From AT

0—Junction with *AT.* Descend steeply, with good winter view, on Old Dug Road.

0.17—White Rocks Trail (see below) intersects on left. Go right at fork just ahead, leaving Old Dug Road.

0.32—Blue-blazed branch trail intersects on left. (It leads to *Bear Spring* in a few yards, then continues to cabin in 0.19 mi., which is half the distance of the main route.) Descend more gradually.

0.55—Several old gullied roads intersect in a small area. *Follow blazes carefully.*

0.59—Bear left off road and onto path.

0.63—Pass stone cellar of house, on right, in profuse growth of periwinkle.

0.70—Bear Spring Cabin. Branch trail rejoins on left. Bear to right of cabin, cross creek, and turn right onto good dirt road.

0.86—As road curves sharply to left, pass pond on right. Ahead, pass trailer on right.

1.04—Junction with Mountain Church Road, beside Locust Valley First Church of God.

WHITE ROCKS TRAIL
Distance 0.28 Mile

Cross-reference: Maryland Section 5 and Bear Spring Cabin Trail

Detailed Trail Data

0—Junction with Bear Spring Cabin Trail. Ascend gradually to foot of quartzite cliff, then scramble very steeply up rocks. *Slippery at all times.*

0.22—View from very small outcrop is poor in summer, but excellent in winter. The prominent ridge in view is South Mountain. This directional illusion is the result of Lambs Knoll being offset to the east from the line of the ridge.

0.28—Junction with *AT.*

GRANT CONWAY TRAIL
Distance 4.62 Miles

This circuit trail is located in the Maryland section of Harpers Ferry National Historical Park, at the southern end of Elk Ridge, across the Potomac from Harpers Ferry. Dedicated to Grant Conway, a former PATC leader, the trail is outstanding for its natural beauty and historic features.

Although relatively short, the trail contains substantial climbs and descents. *Profuse poison ivy,* often overhanging the trail, makes hiking problematic from May through October.

Park regulations prohibit camping and fires. Rock climbers, but not hikers, are required to register with Park rangers in Harpers Ferry.

Cross-reference: Maryland Section 7

Access: Parking is prohibited on Sandy Hook Road. Park at

Harpers Ferry, cross Goodloe Byron Memorial Footbridge, and turn left onto canal towpath. Cross footbridge over canal and cross Sandy Hook Road. *Watch out for traffic.* Trail starts here at old road, marked by "Grant Conway Trail" sign. Distance from *AT* is 0.43 mi.

History Along the Trail

This portion of Elk Ridge, known as Maryland Heights, played an important role in the Civil War. When Lee invaded Maryland in 1862, he detailed Jackson to capture Harpers Ferry. Maryland Heights was abandoned after a short fight by Federal Col. Thomas H. Ford, who was later court-martialed. From these heights, Confederate Major General R.H. Anderson bombarded Harpers Ferry. The garrison surrendered after a short siege, September 13–15.

There are numerous points of historical interest along the trail, mostly on the eastern side of the loop. "Six-Gun Battery" was composed of six 30-pound Parrott siege guns and two 24-pound howitzers. Nearby is the site of the house where Col. Ford made his decision to evacuate Federal troops from the ridge. Farther ahead is "100-Pound Gun." This gun was mounted on a circular track, and Federal gunners once fired it at a stone school house four miles away, demolishing the structure and killing several Confederates within.

The Stone Fort on top of the ridge is constructed of large, shaped blocks of unmortared stone. It was built after 1862 as the anchor to the new Harpers Ferry defense system, and was to be the final refuge for the garrison in the event of another attack. There are parallel walls across the ridge, siege gun positions, three magazines, and low, outer stone walls to protect the infantry. To the northwest, Bakerton and Martinsburg, W.Va., may be seen on clear winter days. To the east are Pleasant Valley and South Mountain.

The signal station for communication with Washington, via Sugar Loaf Mountain and the widow's-walk on the Emory house in Brightwood, is believed to have been located on a high point to the right of the trail. Albert D. Richardson (*Tales of the Secret Service,* 1865) tells of climbing to the signal station and fortifications with a pack train to supply water to troops.

Detailed Trail Data—Naval Battery Branch

0—Sandy Hook Road. Ascend steeply on gated, dirt road, marked by "Grant Conway Trail" sign. Just ahead, turn right off road and onto path. Trail is blazed orange.

0.07—Pass rock outcrop on right which appears to have been chiseled out, perhaps as a probe for ore. Just ahead, house ruins can be seen on left.

0.20—Turn right off road and onto path.

0.40—Naval Battery, built in May 1862, on right. Large earthworks for gun emplacements can be seen. Ahead, turn left.

0.43—Pit on right is "Powder Magazine" according to sign.

0.48—Turn right onto road at junction.

0.53—Junction with loop trail.

Detailed Trail Data—Loop, going clockwise

0.53—Junction with Naval Battery Branch. Turn left and ascend very steeply on old "Military Road."

1.27—Turn right off road and onto path. Ahead, pass earthworks and ammunition pits on both sides of trail.

1.66—Bear right where blue-blazed Elk Ridge Trail intersects on left.

1.71—Cross wall of Stone Fort.

1.74—Pass survey marker for summit of Maryland Heights, 1,475 feet.

2.28—Pass historical marker for "100-Pound Gun." Descend ahead.

2.41—Excellent winter view from rocks on left.

2.56—Pass ammunition pits and infantry defenses on left.

2.71—Unmarked path leads right into "Six-Gun Battery." Turn left.

2.89—Turn right at junction to complete loop. (Trail on left leads 0.48 mi. to Overlook Cliff, with an outstanding view of Harpers Ferry and the rivers.)

3.13—End of loop, at junction with Naval Battery Branch. Total distance, including round-trip to cliff and return to Sandy Hook Road, is 4.62 mi.

Detailed Trail Data—Loop, going counter-clockwise

0.53—Junction with Naval Battery Branch. Go straight and ascend very steeply.

0.77—Turn left onto intersecting trail to continue on loop. (Straight ahead, trail leads 0.48 mi. to Overlook Cliff, with an outstanding view of Harpers Ferry and the rivers.)

0.95—Unmarked path leads straight ahead into "Six-Gun Battery." Turn right.

1.10—Pass ammunition pits and infantry defenses on right.

1.25—Excellent winter view from rocks on right.

1.38—Pass historical marker for "100-Pound Gun."

1.92—Pass survey marker for summit of Maryland Heights, 1,475 feet.

1.95—Cross wall of Stone Fort.

2.00—Bear left where blue-blazed Elk Ridge Trail intersects on right. Ahead, pass earthworks and ammunition pits on both sides of trail.

2.39—Turn left onto old "Military Road" and descend very steeply.

3.13—End of loop, at junction with Naval Battery Branch. Total distance, including round-trip to cliff and return to Sandy Hook Road, is 4.62 mi.

ELK RIDGE TRAIL
Distance 5.78 Miles

This blue-blazed trail is a ridge-walk for most of its length and has one good view. It is also useful for a 20-mile circuit hike, in conjunction with the *AT* and the Grant Conway Trail.

Cross-reference: Grant Conway Trail

Maps: PATC Map #6 and USGS Harpers Ferry and Keedysville Quadrangles

Access: There is no parking on Kaetzell Road. Access is from Grant Conway Trail, or across the valley from Crampton Gap.

History Along the Trail

Elk Ridge was settled during the Revolutionary War by Scottish Highland deserters from the British Army, who later sent for their wives. They were shepherds, gardeners, and weavers by trade, and they earned a living here by truck gardening and charcoal burning for the local iron furnaces. Gradually most of them migrated to the valleys to be closer to other employment. The last settlers were evacuated during the Civil War.

Most of Elk Ridge was included in Samples Manor, a timber holding for charcoal. A narrow-gauge railroad ran along the ridge from near the Stone Fort to Solomons Gap. The horse-drawn coal carts were reversed on a turn-table in Solomons Gap, where the charcoal was transhipped by wagons to Antietam. Coking coal shipped by the Chesapeake & Ohio Canal replaced charcoal at the Antietam Ironworks in the late 1840's, and the rail line was abandoned.

Detailed Trail Data—From Grant Conway Trail

0—Junction with Grant Conway Trail, on northern side of Stone Fort. Trail follows ridge crest with little change in elevation for nearly 2 miles.

2.04—Descend, very steeply at times, on old road.

2.42—Level.

2.47—Go right at fork, off road and onto path.

2.51—Buggy Rocks, on right, has a good view of Pleasant Valley. Trail curves to left, back up hill.

2.62—Trail rejoins road. Turn right.

3.36—Turn right at junction and descend. Solomons Gap is to left.

3.38—Turn right onto dirt road (transcontinental co-axial cable right-of-way) and descend.

3.42—Turn left, off road and onto trail. Ascend very steeply.

3.50—Turn right, onto narrower path, at intersection.

3.66—Top of Gobblers Knob. No view, except through trees when leaves are down. Descend generally ahead, through a series of levels.

4.48—Lots of laurel; pines just ahead.

4.83—Go right at fork onto narrower path in broad, level area. *Easy to miss.*

4.91—Cross old road at sharp angle.

5.24—Cross over headspring for creek.

5.40—Road has gullied into a small stream where it crosses creek. Continue straight across creek. Ruins of a log cabin stand by the creek less than 100 yards downstream.

5.45—Go right at fork, off road and onto path.

5.56—Bear left onto old road at junction. Just ahead, antique wagon stands on left, beside road.

5.65—Go right at fork, off road and onto path.

5.71—Follow right edge of field. Pass to right of barn ahead. This is private property; *stay on trail.*

5.78—Kaetzell Road. Pond on right. Md-67 is 0.98 mi. to left. Crampton Gap is 2.6 mi. via Md-67, Townsend Road, and Md-572 (Gapland Road).

Detailed Trail Data—From Kaetzell Road

0—Kaetzell Road, at 0.98 mi. from Md-67. Ascend along left edge of field, with pond on left. Pass to left of barn ahead. This is private property; *stay on trail.*

0.07—Enter woods.

0.13—Bear left onto intersecting old road.

0.22—Pass antique wagon, on right, beside road. Then go right at fork, off road and onto path.

0.33—Bear left onto intersecting old road.

0.38—Cross creek. Road ahead has gullied into a small stream. Ruins of a log cabin stand by the creek less than 100 yards downstream.

0.54—Cross over headspring of creek.

0.87—Cross old road at sharp angle.

0.95—Bear left onto intersecting trail in broad, level area. Ascend ahead through pine and lots of laurel.

2.12—Top of Gobblers Knob. No view, except through trees when leaves are down. Descend very steeply ahead on narrow path.

2.28—Turn left at junction.

2.36—Turn right onto dirt road (transcontinental co-axial cable right-of-way) and ascend.

2.40—Go left at fork onto old road. (Straight ahead, dirt road leads to Solomons Gap.)

2.42—Turn left at intersection.

3.16—Turn left off road and descend with rocky footing.

3.27—Buggy Rocks, on left, has a good view of Pleasant Valley. Trail curves to right and ascends with better footing.

3.31—Trail rejoins old road. Bear left.

3.36—Ascend, very steeply at times.

3.74—Trail follows ridge crest and eastern rim with little change in elevation to the end.

5.78—Junction with Grant Conway Trail, on northern side of Stone Fort.

VIRGINIA & WEST VIRGINIA
LOUDOUN HEIGHTS TRAIL
Distance 3.19 Miles

This blue-blazed trail follows the former *AT* route past several excellent views and through an historic site in Harpers Ferry National Historical Park. *Park regulations prohibit camping and fires.* In conjunction with the *AT,* it provides a 6.85 mi. circuit hike.

Cross-reference: Maryland Section 7 and Virginia Section 1

Detailed Trail Data—North to South

0—From the *AT* (Maryland Section 7), at the pilings of Sandy Hook Bridge, cross footbridge over canal. Just ahead, cross railroad tracks.

0.04—Sandy Hook (also known, in the 19th century, as Keeptryst Post Office, after the name of a nearby mine). Turn right onto paved Sandy Hook Road. Pass under large highway bridge. Ahead, road has almost no shoulder as it curves. *Exercise great caution.*

0.12—Bear left onto dead-end road (which formerly connected Sandy Hook Road to US-340), cross guard rail, and ascend abandoned road. (To reach the Harpers Ferry Hostel, follow Sandy Hook Road up hill for 0.25 mi. Hostel (with "AYH" sign) occupies house on right, at curve near top of hill.

0.22—Take pedestrian-walk on downstream side of Sandy Hook Bridge (built in 1948), over Potomac River.

0.66—Maryland-Virginia state-line, at south end of Sandy Hook Bridge. Follow US-340 ahead.

0.82—Va-671 intersects on left. Continue on US-340.

1.12—Trail ascends very steeply into woods on left, just beyond end of left guard rail.

1.15—Turn left onto dirt road.

1.27—Turn right off road and onto path just before reaching house. Ascend very steeply by switchbacks, passing several beeches.

1.60—Path on right leads a short distance to Split Rock, which offers a superb view of Elk Ridge and the Potomac River gorge. The trail entered Harpers Ferry National Historical Park just before this point. *Camping and fires are prohibited.* Ahead, steep ascents alternate with level sections as the trail passes through hemlocks to the southeastern side of the ridge.

2.12—Path on right leads a short distance to good view under high-tension powerline.

2.34—Path on right leads a short distance to best view on this trail. (Harpers Ferry, Bolivar, Jefferson Rock, and the rivers are all visible; and the Alleghenies can be seen on a clear day.) Ascend gradually ahead through *profuse poison ivy.*

2.72—Pass rock redoubts dating from the Civil War. (When Lee invaded Maryland in 1862, he detailed Jackson to capture Harpers Ferry, which fell after a short siege, Sept. 13-15. Brigadier General John G. Walker's division bombarded the town from these heights. The redoubts were infantry defenses built and abandoned by the Federals.)

3.19—Junction with the *AT,* in Virginia Section 1.

Detailed Trail Data—South to North

0—From the *AT,* in Virginia Section 1, follow ridge north. This is in Harpers Ferry National Historical Park. *Camping and fires are prohibited.*

0.06—Pass rock redoubts dating from the Civil War. (When Lee invaded Maryland in 1862, he detailed Jackson to capture Harpers Ferry, which fell after a short siege, Sept. 13-15. Brigadier General John G. Walker's division bombarded the town from these heights. The redoubts were infantry defenses built and abandoned by the Federals.) Descend gradually ahead through *profuse poison ivy* in some places.

0.85—Path on left leads a short distance to best view on this trail. (Harpers Ferry, Bolivar, Jefferson Rock, and the rivers are all visible; and the Alleghenies can be seen on a clear day.)

1.07—Path on left leads a short distance to good view under high-tension powerline. Ahead, trail descends steeply at times, through hemlocks, to southeastern side of ridge.

1.59—Path on left leads a short distance to Split Rock, which offers a superb view of Elk Ridge and the Potomac River gorge. Just ahead, the trail leaves Harpers Ferry National Historical Park and descends very steeply by switchbacks, passing several beeches.

1.92—Turn left onto dirt road.

2.04—Turn right off road and onto path.

2.07—Turn right onto US-340.

2.37—Va-671 intersects on right. Continue on US-340.

2.53—Maryland-Virginia state-line. Cross Potomac River by pedestrian-walk, on right side of Sandy Hook Bridge (built in 1948).

2.97—At north end of bridge, proceed parallel to US-340 and descend on abandoned road (which formerly connected US-340 to Sandy Hook Road).

3.07—Bear right onto paved Sandy Hook Road. (To reach the Harpers Ferry Hostel, turn left and follow road for 0.25 mi. Hostel (with "AYH" sign) occupies house on right, at curve near top of hill.) Ahead, road has almost no shoulder as it curves. *Exercise great caution.*

3.15—Sandy Hook (also known, in the 19th century, as Keep-tryst Post Office, after the name of a nearby mine). Turn left off road. Ahead, cross railroad tracks and footbridge over canal.

3.19—Junction with the *AT* (Maryland Section 7), at pilings of Sandy Hook Bridge.

SKY MEADOWS STATE PARK TRAILS
Distance 4.93 Miles

The 1,132 acre Sky Meadows State Park offers a convenient access to the *AT*, a campground, and some short circuit-hikes with extraordinary views from the Park's high meadows. The trails have excellent footing and are also notable for an abundance of dogwood. The Park is open from 8 a.m. to 10 p.m. daily and has a $1.50 entrance fee per car. Beside the parking lot, the Visitor's Center occupies Mt. Bleak Mansion, built about 1820 and once owned by one of Col. Mosby's rangers. In the yard stands the largest Kentucky Coffee-tree in the State: 83 feet high, 7.5 feet wide, and more than 150 years old.

The campground has tent-pads, a shelter, fire-pits, pit-toilets, and a hand-pump well (water *must* be boiled or disinfected, however). Rest rooms are available at the Visitor's Center. The camping fee is $6.00 per site, with a limit of six persons per site. There are no reservations; camping is on a first-come, first-served basis. The ranger comes by to collect fees in the evening. Camping and fires are prohibited elsewhere in the Park.

Cross-reference: Virginia Section 4

Access: From I-66, take US-17 north; or from US-50, take US-17 south. Turn west onto Va-710, the Park entrance road.

North Ridge Trail (blue-blazed)—From Visitor's Center

0—Follow gravel walk west from parking lot.

0.08—Turn left onto gravel road.

0.13—Turn right off road and ascend stairs. (Gap Run Trail goes straight from here.) Just ahead, go straight on gravel path, where Piedmont Overlook Trail intersects on right. Ascend steeply on hillside meadow with outstanding eastward view.

0.30—Bench under hickory tree.

0.46—Cross old stone wall and turn left. Level.

0.56—Ascend into open woods on dirt path.

0.62—Piedmont Overlook Trail intersects on right. Go straight and cross stile. Trail undulates ahead through red oak, hickory, and American basswood.

0.76—Descend steeply.

0.85—Bench. Gap Run Trail intersects on left. Go straight, cross creek just ahead on rock causeway, and ascend, very steeply at times.

1.02—Bear left at fork with old road.

1.41—South Ridge Trail intersects on left. Go straight.

1.73—Junction with *AT,* in Virginia Section 4.

North Ridge Trail (blue-blazed)—From AT

0—Junction with *AT,* in Virginia Section 4. Descend, very steeply at times.

0.32—South Ridge Trail intersects on right. Go straight.

0.71—Bear right onto old road.

0.88—Cross creek on rock causeway and pass Gap Run Trail, which intersects on right. (*AT* hikers should turn right here to reach campground.) Bench. Ascend steeply ahead.

0.97—Trail undulates ahead. Pass some American basswood.

1.11—Piedmont Overlook Trail intersects on left, just past stile. Go straight. Ahead, the trail becomes graveled.

1.27—Turn right and cross old stone wall. Descend steeply on hillside meadow with outstanding eastward view.

1.43—Bench under hickory tree.

1.60—Piedmont Overlook Trail intersects on left. Go straight and turn left onto gravel road ahead.

1.65—Turn right off road and onto gravel walkway.

1.73—Parking lot by Visitor's Center.

Gap Run Trail (orange-blazed)—From Lower End

0—Lower junction with North Ridge Trail, 0.13 mi. from Visitor's Center. Continue straight on gravel road, where North Ridge Trail turns off road to right. Road follows an undulating lane between cow pastures.

0.24—Cross creek.

0.28—Cross stile.

0.34—South Ridge Trail intersects on left. Go straight and ascend through meadow.

0.50—Cross stile and enter woods ahead.

0.57—Cross stream.

0.60—Shelter and picnic tables on right. Privies on left just ahead.

0.62—Well with *non-potable* water, which *must* be boiled or disinfected. Road becomes grassy ahead. Pass tent sites designated by numbered posts.

0.78—Cross creek on rock causeway and ascend steeply.

1.04—Upper junction with North Ridge Trail, at 0.88 mi. from *AT.*

Gap Run Trail (orange-blazed)—From Upper End

0—Upper junction with North Ridge Trail, at 0.88 mi. from *AT.* Descend steeply.

0.26—Cross creek on rock causeway.

0.42—Pass tent sites designated by numbered posts, and pass well with *non-potable* water, which *must* be boiled or disinfected.

0.44—Privies on right. Shelter and picnic tables on left just ahead.

0.47—Cross stream.

0.54—Cross stile and descend through meadow.

0.70—South Ridge Trail intersects on right. Go straight.

0.76—Cross stile. Road forms an undulating lane between cow pastures.

0.80—Cross creek.

1.04—Lower junction with North Ridge Trail, 0.13 mi. from Visitor's Center.

South Ridge Trail (yellow-blazed)—From Lower End

0—Junction with Gap Run Trail.

0.07—Enter woods.

0.14—Pass intersecting path and immense hickory. Ascend very steeply.

0.20—Hillside meadow with outstanding view. There is a bench a short distance up hill straight ahead. Turn left and descend. Ahead, pass path that intersects on left.

0.25—Pass ruins on left and bear right onto old road.

0.28—Pass Snowden Manor ruins on left. Stone chimney, house foundation, and well are visible.

0.34—Turn right and skirt foot of meadow.

0.36—Turn left and ascend very steeply along edge of meadow with outstanding view.

0.49—Bench on left. Bear right around trees ahead.

0.55—Cross stile and enter woods on old road. Generally young forest ahead, with lots of grass and low weeds on each side. Ascend gradually.

1.26—Pass old road that intersects on right.

1.34—Cross stream.

1.59—Junction with North Ridge Trail.

South Ridge Trail (yellow-blazed)—From Upper End

0—Junction with North Ridge Trail. Descend gradually ahead on old road that is rapidly greening over.

0.25—Cross stream.

0.33—Bear right at fork with old road. Generally young forest ahead with lots of grass and low weeds on each side.

1.04—Cross stile and enter hillside meadow with outstanding view. Bear left around trees and skirt left edge of meadow.

1.10—Bench on right. Continue along edge of meadow and descend very steeply.

1.23—Turn right at foot of meadow and skirt edge.

1.25—Turn left into woods and descend on old road.

1.31—Pass Snowden Manor ruins on right. Stone chimney, house foundation, and well are visible.

1.34—Go left at fork off road and onto path. Pass more ruins on right. Ahead, ascend past intersecting path on right.

1.39—Hillside meadow with outstanding view. Bench is a short distance up hill to left. Turn right and descend very steeply into woods along creek.

1.45—Pass immense hickory. Bear right at fork.

1.52—Leave woods on gravel path at foot of meadow.

1.59—Junction with Gap Run Trail.

Piedmont Overlook Trail (red-blazed)—From Lower End

0—Lower junction with North Ridge Trail, at 0.13 mi. from Visitor's Center. Parallel fence.

0.02—Turn left onto road, which curves up to open ridge and disappears. Follow cut path and posts up ridge-meadow.

0.43—Two benches at top of meadow, which has broadest view in Park. Turn left.

0.48—Bear left along fence

0.57—Upper junction with North Ridge Trail, at 1.11 mi. from *AT.*

Piedmont Overlook Trail (red-blazed)—From Upper End

0—Junction with North Ridge Trail, at 1.11 mi. from *AT.* Ascend along fence.

0.09—Bear right away from fence.

0.14—Two benches on hillside meadow, which has broadest view in park. Descend steeply through center of meadow, following cut path and posts. Near bottom, path bears right and turns into a road, which curves back to left beside house.

0.55—Turn right off road and follow fence.

0.57—Lower junction with North Ridge Trail, at 0.13 mi. from Visitor's Center.

CHAPTER 8
SHELTERS

Hikers of this section of the *AT* are fortunate in having well-built and attractively located shelters that are an easy-to-moderate day's walk apart. Hikers will find that they often have the opportunity to choose their shelters according to the distance they prefer to hike.

These shelters are three-sided structures with raised wooden floors (except for Hodgson House; see Virginia Section 2). Most have fireplaces and pit-toilets. (Exceptions are noted in the Trail sections.) The shelters at Hemlock Hill and Keys Gap have no nearby water available. The spring at Rocky Run is seasonal.

Shelters are open to hikers for free on a first-come, first-served basis, *but early arrivals should admit late-comers up to the capacity of the shelter.* Users are expected not to deface the shelters, tables, fireplaces, etc., and they should carry out all of their trash.

There is currently an epidemic of rabies, particularly among raccoons, in Maryland and northern Virginia. Leaving behind garbage or unused food, which attracts animals, is now especially hazardous to the welfare of other hikers. For more on the rabies problem, see Chapter 1.

Caution should be used at all times with fires, which should be confined to the fireplaces and never left untended. Fires should be out to the last spark before hikers leave the shelter.

Firewood is a problem near most of the shelters, but a little scouting through the woods generally will turn up enough dry wood. In no event are standing trees (live or dead) to be cut or defaced. Hikers also are asked to leave a small supply of dry wood inside for others, who may arrive late at night or in a storm. The courtesy will be returned.

On the following list, the distances shown are from the preceding shelter, north to south. Distances do not include the length of the shelter-access trails.

State & Section	*Shelter*	*Distance*
Maryland		
1	Devils Racecourse	7.37
3	Hemlock Hill	4.63
3	Pine Knob	8.08
5	Rocky Run	7.16
5	Crampton Gap	5.15
Virginia/ West Virginia		
2	Keys Gap	16.83
2	Hodgson House	6.29
3	Rod Hollow	17.29
4	Dick's Dome	8.90
4	Manassas Gap	4.68
5	Linden	5.54
6	Tom Floyd Wayside	8.67
(SNP)	(Gravel Springs)	(9.94)

Pine Knob Shelter

INDEX

This index covers only place names and road crossings that pertain to the Trail and side trails. Blue Ridge, South Mountain, states, and counties are excluded.

NOTES

NOTES